Fundamentals of Criminal Justice Research

Stephen E. Brown
John H. Curtis

PILGRIMAGE
A Division Of Anderson Publishing Co.
Cincinnati, Ohio

 Criminal Justice Studies

FUNDAMENTALS OF CRIMINAL JUSTICE RESEARCH
© copyright 1987 by Anderson Publishing Co.

ISBN: 0-932930-73-5

Cover design by Ross Heck

 Criminal Justice Studies
Anderson Publishing Co./Cincinnati, Ohio

Contents

Preface

Fundamentals of Criminal Justice Research is offered to undergraduate and graduate students in criminal justice to serve as a roadmap to the design and completion of a basic research project. It is designed for use as a text in applied criminal justice research courses or as a supplementary text to augment more traditional courses for which an applied dimension is sought. Its purpose is to enhance the application of research skills rather than to provide the foundation for understanding statistics and research methods. When *Fundamentals of Criminal Justice Research* is used, a student should be able to complete a basic research project during a typical college term in conjunction with lectures and other assigned readings. It is structured to guide the student through the following phases of a research project:
- conceptualizing the research problem
- developing a related body of theory
- designing a data collection instrument
- collecting and analyzing the data
- reporting finding to the criminal justice discipline

We extend our gratitude to Sharon Elliott for manuscript typing and other assistance in the preparation of this book. Her support during this endeavor was invaluable. We would also like to thank Michael Braswell for his encouragement to undertake and complete this project. We acknowledge permission from SPSS Inc. to use their SPSS-X software package*. Ideal Systems extended permission for the use of INTROSTAT 2.2 in chapter 5. Additionally, we appreciate the permission of the National Council on Crime and Delinquency to include materials. The Office of Computing and Information Resources at East Tennessee State University provided computer support. Finally, we thank the many students of research whom the authors have taught and learned from over the years. We hope that this text will help students in the field of criminal justice to learn about the research process.

Stephen E. Brown
Department of Criminal Justice
East Tennessee State University

John H. Curtis
Department of Sociology
and Anthropology
Valdosta State College

*SPSS-X is a trademark of SPSS Inc. of Chicago, Illinois, for its proprietary computer software.

1

Criminal Justice Research: An Introduction and Overview

Building research skills requires that attention be simultaneously focused on two constituents of the research process: research design (often called methodology or simply methods) and analysis. The analytical phase of research involves the application of statistics whenever the data generated by the research design are in a quantitative form. But the very sound of the terms *research* and *statistics* have an unsettling effect on many criminal justice and other social science students. A review of introductory pages to general social science research and statistics texts reveals an array of adjectives describing the feelings of many students: anxiety, apprehension, distaste, and fear. Hagan (1982:1), in the opening line of his text, *Research Methods in Criminal Justice and Criminology,* observes: "Most students of criminal justice approach a course in research methods with the enthusiasm of a recalcitrant patient in a dentist's office." Frequently the required research course is viewed as an obstacle to completion of degree requirements. The most common explanation is *math anxiety* or *math avoidance,* a widespread problem recently identified by Tobias (1980). Students often associate research with math, hence entering their research classes with anxiety, apprehension, and fear.

Fundamentals of Criminal Justice Research does not take a mathematical approach to research. This text incorporates an applied approach (Brown, 1981) that will involve you with a hands-on research experience with minimal technical understanding of statistics. It is designed to guide you completely through a research project. It is a learning-by-doing approach that has been found to be an excellent technique for students in many criminal justice and other social science programs (Brown, 1981). Dismiss any research anxiety you might feel; select a research topic that interests you and enjoy your research experience. It can be one of your most rewarding endeavors as a criminal justice student.

Next to an anxiety response, the most common objection that criminal justice students have about their research course is the need or relevance of studying research. A *common sense* myth maintaining that solutions to criminal justice problems require only the application of common sense is widespread in the field. But common sense is so often nonsense! Common sense is not a sufficient, though it may be a necessary, tool for discovering knowledge about crime and criminal justice responses to it. Many practitioners within criminal justice have met with repeated failure over the years because they relied upon only their common sense. Thus, millions of dollars have been spent on police patrol efforts that do not reduce crime, judicial practices that are widely perceived as unfair, rehabilitation programs that do not rehabilitate offenders and countless other failures. All of the problems that cause crime or how to always best respond will probably never be fully understood. Research is and will continue to be our primary means of learning answers to these questions.

Criminal justice research involves the application of the scientific method to answer previously unsolved questions or problems relating to crime and the criminal justice system. It is this research process that generates the knowledge upon which the successful operation of criminal justice systems depends. The consequences of missing this important point means continued failures for the criminal justice system. Moreover, if the various criminal justice roles are to develop as professions, it is necessary to continuously add to a body of scientific knowledge, and criminal justice professionals must be able to digest that body of knowledge and the scientific procedures through which it has evolved.

Aside from the fact that research serves as the predominant tool for acquiring knowledge about criminal justice, there are also practical reasons for studying criminal justice research. First, as a criminal justice professional, you may be involved with research as a consumer, a supervisor of research producers and/or as a researcher yourself. As a professional consumer you should be able to read and understand research reports to take advantage of the findings to better serve your clientele and your community. As a supervisor of personnel, for example in the planning and research unit of a criminal justice agency, you should be capable of evaluating the evaluators. All research is not equal and you should have enough knowledge of research to discern the products in terms of quality. Finally, your education will render you a logical candidate for evaluation research within an agency. Over the years, the authors have had numerous students return and express relief that they knew how to go about organizing a research project that they had been assigned to undertake in a criminal justice agency. It is this experience that *Fundamentals of Criminal Justice Research* is designed to provide.

Another rationale for the study of research is that it is a fundamental element of the complex contemporary world. You cannot escape making decisions regarding life-style. What kinds of foods will you eat? What forms of birth control will you use? What forms of medication will you take? Will you smoke? Will you allow others to smoke in your presence? Important life-style decisions require personal decisions based upon knowledge generated by scientific research. The knowledge of risks associated with products or activities must be weighed against certain values. Research cannot address values, but it is the only way to assess objective questions, such as the risk of undesirable side-effects that can be rendered by use of a product. More informed decisions will be the result if you understand the process by which knowledge was discovered. Those lacking an understanding of the research process often respond to new research findings with extreme reactions. Either they are skeptical of all discoveries and attempt to rationalize dangerous behaviors (*e.g.,* "My granddaddy smoked and lived to be 92) or they panic and continually overreact to new findings (*e.g.,* "I disposed of every aerosol spray in my house so I would not destroy the ozone layer.") Both extremes reflect a misunderstanding of research and contribute to poor decisions. The smoker did not understand that research has not indicated that all smokers will die prematurely of cancer, emphysema or heart disease, but rather that the risk of premature death and disability is significantly and substantially increased. One smoking granddaddy establishes nothing, whether he died of lung cancer at 29 or in a barroom brawl at 92. Conversely, the aerosol panic was eccentric at best since the original research suggested only a gradual impact on the ozone layer over decades of world-wide usage and later research discounted these findings. Thus, our research-ignorant person disposed of his/her deodorant unnecessarily, possibly with some unpleasant results.

The Scientific Method

Criminal justice research is the application of the scientific method to answer previously unsolved questions or problems relating to crime and the criminal justice system. The scientific method is the most widely accepted means for seeking truth or knowledge in contemporary society. Criminal justice has emerged in recent years as one of the most exciting social sciences. As with any science, there are two major components: the theoretical and the empirical. The scientific process can begin with theory and then proceed to empirical testing, a process referred to as deductive. Conversely, the process can be initiated by empirical observations which are then incorporated into a body of theory. This is the inductive method. It is very important to understand that the theoretical and the empirical are interfaces of the process of knowledge creation. Research establishes facts; facts are then organized into theories; theories generate new hypotheses to be tested; new facts are established by tests. A circular paradigm is implied in which research and theory feed each other. So goes the scientific method. Figure 1.1 illustrates the scientific method and the interface between the theoretical and empirical components.

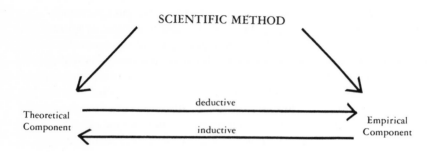

Figure 1.1 Components of the Scientific Method

Let's take an overview of the scientific method as it will be presented in this text to guide you through your own research project. First you must identify what you want to study. Many students find this to be difficult, but nobody else can select a research area for you since the single most important criteria in making the selection is that the topic interest you. You need to select a topic that you have a real desire to learn about and then employ the scientific method as your tool for learning. Initially, you may not have a research question, but only a general topical area. If this is the case, a literature review of the subject will help you to formulate a researchable question or hypothesis. Chapter 2 addresses the literature review process. It will reveal what research has already been conducted on your topic and what questions have not previously been addressed by research. You may elect to conduct research to try finding an answer to some question that is currently unknown or you may decide to replicate previous research. While a replication does not produce new knowledge, it is helpful to confirm the adequacy of previous research. It may be done exactly the same as the original research or it may incorporate new methods.

The literature review will also help you develop a theoretical understanding of your topic. Since your research will most likely be initiated by deductive thinking, this is an important step in developing logical explanations for the way things are. Your efforts at theorizing are of little value if your ideas are already represented in the literature, so see what ideas have already been developed. There is no need to reinvent the wheel. After you have digested the ideas in the literature, ask what you can add. Can you improve those theories? If they are unconfirmed theories, plan to test them by doing research. Remember, theory development is only part of science. What you will be doing is testing your theory or ideas by conducting empirical research.

After conducting your literature review and developing a body of theory, you will derive a *hypothesis* or series of hypotheses from your theoretical framework. The hypothesis is a testable statement or prediction as to what patterns you will observe in the data you collect. Each hypothesis consists, implicitly or explicitly, of a null and an alternative (often called research) hypothesis. Be sure that your hypothesis contains two variables and that they are stated in measurable terms.

The next step is to develop a methodology for collecting the data that will be used in testing your hypothesis. Most popular among student researchers are survey designs that utilize questionnaires. This method is emphasized in Chapter 3. Other data sources include experiments, participant observation, interviews and many more techniques. Another important aspect of the research methodology is the identification of the population you wish to study and a *sampling* strategy. You will study the sample and draw inferences to the population, a practice that is justified by random or other representative sampling techniques. Finally, be sure that your *unit of analysis* is clear. A given hypothesis can be tested with observations made for different units of analysis. For example, the variable *crime* could be quantified by counting the number in a sample of persons who have committed offenses. Crime could also be quantified by counting the number of crimes in a geographic area. Thus, we could study the relationship between crime and social class by comparing rates of criminal offenses among lower versus middle class persons or by comparing crime rates in lower versus middle class neighborhoods. So entirely distinct data sources are available to address the same or similar research questions.

Once the data are collected they will be subjected to analysis. Quantitative data will be analyzed by the application of statistical methods, while qualitative researchers must develop their own analytical schemes. The computer is an indispensable tool in most quantitative research because it dramatically increases both the speed and accuracy of analyses. Chapter 4 reviews major analytical techniques for quantitative research, while use of the computer as a tool is examined in Chapter 5.

Your completed data analysis feeds back to your original theory resulting in ideas that are confirmed, rejected or modified as a consequence of the research findings. Thus, the scientific process is generally continuous and circuitous, though this is more so for basic or pure research than for applied research. This theory revision will complete your scientific project though it probably will suggest a need for further research. The final chapter of this text will guide you in the oral and written presentation of your research.

Quantitative Versus Qualitative Research

There are two basic approaches to research methods: quantitative and qualitative. Both are important and both are needed in criminal justice research. Quantitative research is the more traditional of the two methods. It refers to the counting mechanisms that organize and describe phenomena statistically. Quantitative researchers are noted for their use of the computer and statistical techniques. In addition, quantitative research dominates the publishing field and provides the primary focus for this text. Some persons suggest that one of these two methods is better than the other, but this is misleading. They are both important methods that may be complementary, but more importantly, they usually apply to different research situations. Generally, qualitative research is appropriate at an exploratory level. That is, if little is known about a topic it is probably more appropriate to plan a qualitative methodology. Conversely, quantitative research requires a more developed understanding of the research problems.

Quantitative research is often dependent on the computer. The computer makes it possible to count faster and more accurately. Math models can be programmed so that rather sophisticated techniques can be used in a relatively short duration of time. Statistical tests of significance allow for the making of inferences from samples to populations. Various correlational tests allow the quantitative researcher to suggest the strength of trends. New models emerge that seem to be more predictive. However conceived, the process of counting has become a science.

Let's look at an example for purposes of contrasting qualitative and quantitative research. Suppose you are interested in conducting research on police dispatching. The first thing you would do is conduct a literature review to see what ideas and data are already available. What if you did a thorough search and found very little description of what takes place in a police communication center? Yet you want to know about who calls, why they call, how dispatchers respond to calls, how they acquire the necessary information from excited callers, how they prioritize calls when insufficient numbers of patrol units are available to service all calls at a given time and so forth. If the literature does not provide a good overview of police dispatching from which you could derive hypotheses that could be quantitatively tested, then a qualitative research design would probably be most appropriate.

There are numerous variations of qualitative methods. The life study approach involves the acquisition of a life history from subjects and is illustrated by Shaw's *The Jackroller* (1968) which related the story of his subject, "Stanley," and his involvement in delinquency and then crime. Another extremely interesting work generated by the same method is Klockars' *The Professional Fence* (1974) in which the fencing activities and techniques of "Vincent" are chronicled. Participant observation is probably the most common qualitative approach. It is represented by such classics as Malinowski's *Crime and Custom in Savage Society* (1969) and Thrasher's *The Gang* (1963). Participant observation studies are usually exciting to read as well as to undertake. However, grave ethical questions emerge concerning just how involved a participant observer should be and how honest he should be in revealing the research motivation for his presence. Humphreys' (1970) study, entitled *Tearoom Trade*, became widely known for the deceit exercised by the researcher in playing the role of "watchqueen" during homosexual encounters in public restrooms. He observed many men engaging in deviant sexual acts under the guise of being a voyeur, then he recorded their license plate numbers, disguised himself and sought permission to interview them in their homes, again under false pretenses! Thompson (1967) rode with the Hell's Angels as a participant observer and although he was honest with his subjects from the beginning, was eventually rewarded for his research efforts with a severe beating.

One thing that should be evident is that qualitative research is more exciting and emotion-arousing for most persons than is quantitative research. It may be a special breed of person who gets excited about tests of statistical significance that are reported on a computer printout, but most of us will find many qualitative studies to be tremendously provocative. Of course you may prefer a "safer" (often literally) approach to the study of crime and criminal justice. But if you aspire to "exciting" research, why not take the qualitative route? You may want to do so, but another caution is in order. Contrary to what the research neophyte often expects, qualitative research actually requires far more research skill and knowledge than is the case for quantitative designs. Quantitative techniques insure scientific rigor and their implementation is relatively straightforward. Not so for qualitative research! The qualitative researcher is much more on his/her own during both research design and analysis. There are countless biases and errors that can circumvent qualitative research efforts. In contrast, statistical models control for many of these problems in quantitative research. The qualitative researcher has the sole responsibility for the accurate presentation of the findings and must construct analytical categories which make the entire effort comprehensible to others. Also, the qualitative researcher is responsible to make him or herself available to the criticisms of other researchers. In the final report there must be a detailed description of how the researcher went about mapping out the problem. This is similar to the "Methods" section of a quantitative paper. Biases must be stated explicitly. Problems in conducting the research must be articulated. The "nuts and bolts" of the research activity must be presented so that there is a clear distinction between qualitative research and social journalism.

In summary, qualitative research can be especially interesting and exciting. However, quantitative designs are recommended for the beginning researcher because the structure provided will facilitate the scientific approach. For this reason, *Fundamentals of Criminal Justice Research* focuses upon quantitative research designs.

References

Brown, Stephen E. "Research Methods and Criminal Justice Curricula: Surmounting the Obstacles" (1981) *Criminal Justice Review* 7:11-16.

Hagan, Frank E. *Research Methods in Criminal Justice and Criminology* (New York: Macmillan, 1982).

Humphreys, Laud *Tearoom Trade* (Chicago: Aldine Publishing Company, 1975).

Klockars, Carl B. *The Professional Fence* (New York: The Free Press, 1974).

Malinowski, Branislaw *Crime and Custom in Savage Society* (New Jersey: Littlefield, Adams and Company, 1969).

Shaw, Clifford *The Jack-Roller* (Chicago: The University of Chicago Press, 1968).

Thompson, Hunter *Hell's Angels* (New York: Ballantine Books, 1967).

Thrasher, Frederic M. *The Gang* (Chicago: The University of Chicago Press, 1963).

Tobias, Sheila *Overcoming Math Anxiety* (Boston: Houghton Mifflin, 1980).

2
Getting Started

Before actually getting your research underway, there are several preparatory steps you must take. Remember that the scientific method is comprised of two basic components: the theoretical and the empirical. So before actually initiating empirical research, you ordinarily (*i.e.*, with the deductive approach) should develop an extensive theoretical underpinning. Doing this requires that you conduct a literature review and then critically evaluate the existing literature. Once you have a grasp of the literature on your topic and know where you can provide some increment in knowledge, it is time to develop a proposal. This chapter discusses the literature review, literature critique and proposal stages of your scientific project.

The Literature Review

One of the skills essential to planning good research is that of conducting a sound literature review. It is the theory development and research conceptualization resulting from the literature review that provides the foundation for the research. Obviously, good research requires the development of good theory, and to cultivate theory you must know what good references are, how to locate and how to use them. References basically fall into two categories: books and periodicals (journals). In conducting a literature review of a particular topic, you should exhaust both categories.

Books

For research purposes, introductory level textbooks are generally not acceptable. They are written to introduce students to their subject matter and do not have sufficient depth. They might be used as a starting point to direct you to *primary references* , but should not serve as major references to support your literature review. Instead, go to the original sources cited in textbooks. If entire books devoted specifically to your topic are available, they should be used. The extent to which you rely on such books will vary according to their quality, date of publication, the availability of journal articles and other factors. Another type of book which may be a useful source is the edited variety (often called readers). These are collections of articles on a range of topics which have been brought together by an editor who sometimes writes introductory sections for each group of articles in the book. Sometimes these articles are reprinted from journals and sometimes they are original contributions.

In order to locate relevant books, the researcher must understand the classification system used in libraries. One system that has been popular in the past is the *Dewey Decimal System* . In this system, numerical coefficients give the researcher direction to the works of a given discipline. For example, the writings in the social sciences are numbered in the 300's. A newer system is the *Library of Congress Classification System* which uses both letters and numbers to guide the researcher to a given book. Students need to be familiar with both systems in order to effectively use most libraries. Many libraries are in a state of transition changing their catalogue system from the Dewey to the Library of Congress System.

The Dewey Decimal System

000	General Works
100	Philosophy
200	Religion
300	Social Science
301	Sociology
310	Statistics
360	Social Services
364	Criminal Justice
400	Languages
500	Science and Mathematics
572	Anthropology
600	Applied Sciences
700	Fine Arts and Recreation
800	Literature
900	History, Travel, and Biography

The Library of Congress Classification System

Twenty-one main classes of books are identified by letters and/or combinations of letters. The social scientist will want to be familiar with:

G	Geography, Anthropology, and Folklore
H	Social Sciences (Sociology, Economics)
J	Political Science

The addition of a second letter denotes subdivisions within each category. For example:

HM	Sociology: General Works, Theory
HQ-HT	Social Groups
HT	Communities, Classes, Races

Further subdivisions are made by adding numbers to the letter codes so that HQ 1381 refers to "Women and Economics."

Students should be aware that materials in most books will be outdated for a research report. By the time an article is included in a book it is typically over five years dated. For this reason students should regularly scan the journals for references in the literature review. With the exception of benchmark (world famous) studies, the student typically can limit his or her review of the literature to the previous decade.

Occasionally a student will research a topic in which there is no body of related studies. In such a situation the student should look for literature that complements the broad definition of his or her problem. If this is followed, it should always be possible to find ten articles from books, micromaterials, and journals for the review of the literature.

Whenever works older than the previous decade are cited, they should represent a standard work of the field. Examples of these classics in some different areas of criminal justice are: Wolfgang's (1958) *Patterns of Criminal Homicide,* Sutherland's (1949) *White-Collar Crime,* Cohen's (1955) *Delinquent Boys,* Skolnick's (1966) *Justice Without Trial* and Niederhoffer's (1967) *Behind the Shield.* For most topics of study there will be one or more definitive works that have set the standard for further research. Not to cite such a work is as much an oversight as it is to miss a relevant journal article just published in the latest edition.

Journals

The professional journals in criminal justice, criminology and related social sciences provide access to the most current theory and research of the field. There are many journals that may publish articles relevant to any particular criminal justice topic, although they vary widely in terms of the quality of the works published. A sound literature review requires the researcher to develop a bibliography based upon an exhaustive review of all of these journals for the most recent five years while also including any older articles that are classics. You may find the research reported in some of these journals to be difficult to comprehend. The articles may require outlining and/or reading a second or third time. However, this effort will be rewarding as you will become more proficient at digesting the professional literature of the criminal justice field. As Hagan (1982:4) has pointed out, "it is imperative that criminal justice professionals comprehend and critically evaluate new developments in their field." Unfortunately, he also observes that "it is not unusual to find students as well as professionals and administrators in criminal justice who are unable to fully understand reports and journal articles in their own field."

The following is a list of journals that publish articles in the field of criminal justice, though by no means is it an exhaustive listing.

American Journal of Police
American Journal of Sociology
American Sociological Review
British Journal of Criminology
California Youth Authority Quarterly
Canadian Journal of Criminology
Crime and Delinquency
Crime and Social Justice
Criminal Justice and Behavior
Criminal Justice Review
Criminology
International Journal of Criminology and Penology
International Journal of Offender Therapy and Comparative
  Criminology
International Journal of the Sociology of Law
Journal of Crime and Justice
Journal of Criminal Justice
Journal of Criminal Law and Criminology
Journal of Legal Studies
Journal of Police and Criminal Psychology
Journal of Police Science and Administration
Journal of Quantitative Criminology
Journal of Research in Crime and Delinquency
Justice Quarterly
Law and Society Review
Police Chief
Police Studies
Police Studies Journal
Social Forces
Social Problems
Social Science Quarterly
Sociological Inquiry
Southern Journal of Criminal Justice

Victimology
Youth and Society

   With the criminal justice literature spread through these and many other journals, the researcher must have some tool to facilitate a systematic review. These tools are the sets of abstracts that enable the researcher to develop a complete bibliography for a subject in a short period of time. Without them, there would be no means of accomplishing a thorough literature review in a reasonable time frame. One of the frequent, but very serious mistakes of beginning researchers is to attempt to undertake the literature review without carefully working through the abstracts. An adequate literature review simply cannot be conducted without them.

   Abstracts typically are published six times annually. The most recent volume (year) will be in separate unbound issues while the earlier volumes are bound. To employ the abstracts in locating references, make a list of all relevant terms for your subject. Then look up these topics in the subject index in back of the most recent issue of the current volume and repeat this working back through all preceding issues. Then go to the cumulative index of the most recent bound volume and again look up these subjects. Work backward through the bound volumes as far as necessary. Each time you locate a reference that may be appropriate, turn to the abstract which is indicated by the number in the index. Read the abstract to determine if it is relevant to your topic. If so, record all bibliographic information so that you can locate it in the library. There is an author index if you need to locate the writings of a particuar author. In undertaking the literature review, some of the following sets of abstracts should be utilized.

   Abstracts on Criminology and Penology
   Abstracts on Police Science
   Crime and Delinquency Abstracts
   Criminal Justice Abstracts
   Psychological Abstracts
   Social Science Index
   Sociological Abstracts

   Not every journal is included in every abstract service. You need to select the most appropriate sets of abstracts to review for your subject. Even then you will need to employ some other methods of finding journal articles. However, the abstracts will almost always be the single most important tool in the literature review.

Critiquing Journal Articles

Once the bibliography of journal articles is developed there are some helpful hints for their effective use. When you first look at a journal, scan the titles of the articles and the abstracts. The primary variables explored in the article are probably incorporated in the title. If not, they will certainly be found in the abstract. This is an effective screening device. Then read the discussion sections from those articles that are germane to your research. When you have narrowed the total number of articles to those that appear to have a relevance to your subject, read those articles carefully. When you have read the article carefully ask the following questions:

1. Was the problem statement apparent?
2. Was the problem related to a theoretical frame of reference?
3. Were the analyses adequately explained?
4. Were the conclusions tied to empirical evidence?
5. Did the article make an argument that seemed to be logical?

With these questions you have started the process of critiquing a journal article. This is important as every student must be able to distinguish between poorly written and designed articles and those whose findings can be accepted as reliable. Every student should be warned that just because an article is in print does not necessarily mean it is reliable. Consequently, the student must use caution when accepting conclusions even though they appear in a professional journal.

When reading and critiquing a journal article there are always certain key points to examine. Dr. A. W. Melton at Valdosta State College, asks students to review five components as follows when analyzing an article:

Brief Critique

1. *Citation*. The bibliographic reference of the article.
2. *Purpose*. The problem studied, its relevance, the theoretical frame of reference, and the basic reference cited from previous research.
3. *Project Development*. The method of inquiry including such information as the group or area studied, the rationale for the research design, the procedures, and the construction of the data gathering instrument. If a published test is used to collect data, then there should be an explanation of its strengths and the results that can be expected from it.
4. *Findings*. The presentation of the conclusions from the study.

5. *Critique.* The student's scholarly evaluation of the investigation and
the results. Be sure to set forth the limitations of the
study and its difficulties. Then discuss the strengths of
the study and how it might have been improved. Finally
discuss the social implications of the research in terms
of theory, social relevance, and its worth to society.

This critique format is brief and to the point. It should help the student
quickly organize the research notes so as to be able to present a discussion
of an article in class or in a written paper.

A more extensive outline that will yield the same information may
sometimes be needed. When the student wants to do an in-depth critique,
the following outline for research evaluation should prove valuable. The
student may feel the need to complete all of this outline or to choose
among items that are the most relevant to his or her research review.

Extended Critique

1. *The Problem*
A. What is the social issue being studied?
B. What is the research problem?
C. Identify the Independent Variable(s).
D. Identify the Dependent Variable(s).
E. What relationship between the Variables has been hypothesized?
F. Was the hypothesis testable?
G. What was the theoretical frame of reference for the problem?
H. How was previous research brought to bear on the formation of the
   research problem?

2. *The Method*
A. Was there a clearly developed research design?
B. What method of sampling was used?
C. Was the sampling method adequate?
D. Were the subjects described?
E. Were they representative of the population?
F. Can generalizations be made from the sample to the population?
G. Were the procedures developed from the theoretical frame of
   reference?
H. Were the procedures clearly stated so that replication might be
   possible? Could you replicate this study if you chose to do so?
I. Were the measurement techniques valid and reliable?
J. Were the procedures implemented?

3. *The Findings*

A. How were the data summarized?

B. Were the tables logical and clear?

C. Were the statistical techniques appropriate?

D. Would other statistical techniques have been more appropriate?

E. Did the findings relate to the problem, the method, and/or the theoretical framework?

F. How were these findings related to the findings of other independent researchers?

4. *Dissemination*

A. How have these findings been reported to the professional and general public?

B. Could these findings have been made available to the public in any other manner?

5. *Research Ethics*

A. Were ethical guidelines strictly followed especially in the use of human and/or animal subjects?

B. Were the project design and instruments approved by the appropriate review committees?

C. Were the subjects given appropriate feedback concerning the findings?

6. *Social Significance*

A. Did these findings or the specific application of this method contribute to the well-being of mankind?

B. Did the findings amplify scientific method, theory, or knowledge?

C. Was this study socially relevant? Why?

When you have completed this more extensive critique format, you have have an in-depth understanding of the total project. Such an understanding will allow the incorporation of findings from the study in your literature review.

A third format for critiquing articles will prove useful in helping to understand methodologies and plan for your own. You should be able to complete the following ten-item critique of any empirical studies found in the literature review.

Methodological Critique

1. What was the method of observation or data collection?

2. What was the unit of analysis?

3. What was the hypothesis or what were the hypotheses?
4. For each hypothesis, what were the independent, dependent and control variables?
5. What were the categories or attributes of each variable?
6. What were the indicators or mode of operationalization for each variable?
7. What was the level of measurement for each variable?
8. What statistical tests were employed for each hypothesis?
9. What were the findings in terms of patterns in the data for each hypothesis?
10. Identify the greatest strengths and weaknesses in the research design and analysis.

The Proposal

Before initiating your research project, a research proposal should be developed. This proposal may need to be submitted to the appropriate college or university committees prior to conducting the research project. For this reason it is always wise to prepare a formal proposal. The following guidelines should help the student understand and develop the component parts of a research proposal.

In any research the major emphasis must be on the construction of the research design. This is always accomplished before any data are collected. While the research student generally enjoys gathering data, the data may be useless unless there is an adequate design. A research proposal is a summary of the research problem, design, and the instruments to be used in data collection. The data collection instrument should be affixed to the research proposal and data should not be gathered until the proposal is approved by the appropriate committees and signed. Note that the research proposal is always written in the future tense. It should be written in clear and concise terms. It need not be lengthy and detailed, but rather should be thought of as an "incomplete map of the research territory" (Johnson, 1981:42). The following is a suggested outline for the proposal:

1. Title
2. Purpose
3. Theoretical Framework
4. Hypotheses
5. Methodology
      A. Unit of Analysis
      B. Means of Data Collection
      C. Sampling
      D. Instrument(s)

        E. Statistics
        F. Computer Hardware and Software
    6. Time Frame
    7. Ethical Issues
    8. Bibliography

Exercises

1. List the sets of criminal justice and other social science abstracts available in your library. For what years are they available?

2. Use two sets of abstracts to generate a bibliography of at least ten journal articles on a subject of your choice.

3. Which classification system is used for books in your library?

4. Use your card catalog to develop a bibliography of at least five books on a subject of your choice.

5. Develop a list of the journals listed in this chapter that are available in your library.

6. Select one or more journal articles and prepare the brief, extended and methodological critiques outlined in this chapter.

7. Prepare a proposal for a research project.

References

Cohen, Albert K. *Delinquent Boys: The Culture of the Gang* (New York: The Free Press, 1955).

Hagan, Frank E. *Research Methods in Criminal Justice and Criminology* (New York: Macmillan, 1982).

Johnson, Edwin S. *Research Method in Criminology and Criminal Justice* (New Jersey: Prentice-Hall, 1981).

Niederhoffer, Arthur *Behind the Shield: The Police in Urban Society* (New York: Doubleday and Company, Inc., 1967).

Skolnick, Jerome *Justice Without Trial* (New York: John Wiley and Sons, Inc., 1966).

Sutherland, Edwin H. *White Collar Crime* (New York: Holt, Rinehart and Winston, 1949).

Wolfgang, Marvin E. *Patterns in Criminal Homicide* (New Jersey: Patterson Smith, 1975).

3

Data Collection Instruments

Criminal justice researchers use a variety of data collection instruments in the research process. An important task of the researcher is to adopt or construct a valid and reliable data gathering instrument. Remember that a valid instrument is one that measures the intended underlying concept, while a reliable one consistently yields the same results if all else remains constant. There are four major forms of data collection.

First is the questionnaire. The questionnaire is popular because it allows for the collection of a wide variety of data from subjects with relative ease and economy. They may be administered in a variety of surroundings (*e.g.,* mailed, assembled groups, as part of established procedures with criminal justice system clientele, etc.) and formats (*e.g.,* open or close ended, attitude scales, perceptual questions, vignettes, etc.). A very important feature of the questionnaire is that it can be used to collect relatively sensitive data, as much of interest to us in criminal justice is, by assuring confidentiality or anonymity. It is best to collect anonymous data whenever possible to protect both the respondent and the researcher.

The interview schedule is a second form of data collection. With this instrument, the researcher orally communicates questions to subjects and then records the responses. This is often done via telephone using random digit dialing techniques. It can also be conducted in person. It is used less often than the questionnaire because it is much more time consuming and ordinarily an inappropriate technique for collecting sensitive data. Also, reliability is more difficult to establish because responses must be interpreted by the interviewer before recording.

The use of secondary data is very common in criminal justice. These are existing data that can be marshalled by the researcher to address their research questions without having to collect original data. Economy is a major advantage and making frequent use of existing data, especially by student researchers, helps to prevent criminal justice agencies from being saturated with research activities. The major drawback is that the available data ordinarily have not been collected to address the specific questions of the researcher. Nevertheless secondary data are a very practical choice for student researchers in particular.

The test instrument is the fourth major form of data collection. Many published tests are available that feature substantial reliability and validity data. They are most common in the psychology and education literature, but are frequently useful in criminal justice research.

Sample Instruments

This section presents some sample instruments for each of the four major forms of data collection. One of the first decisions you must make in a research undertaking is whether you can use an existing instrument or must undertake the task of instrument development. The literature review should reveal what is available and it will be very helpful if you can adopt or adapt an existing instrument.

Questionnaires

The first example of an existing scale for inclusion in questionnaires is a Child Maltreatment Scale (Brown, 1984). This scale employed predominantly Likert-type response categories for items that actually comprise three subscales. Thus, three variations of child maltreatment can be measured by including these items on a questionnaire and they can serve as independent or dependent variables depending on the researcher's hypotheses. The scale can be used to measure maltreatment by parents or by the father and mother individually. Note also that the instrument is designed for administration to youth, but could be modified for use with adults. The items should be mixed up in the questionnaire rather than presented in separate blocks.

CHILD MALTREATMENT SCALE

Neglect

How often do you eat supper with your parents?
never   rarely   sometimes   usually   always

How often do you miss meals?
Breakfast:
never   rarely   sometimes   usually   always
Lunch:
never   rarely   sometimes   usually   always
Supper:
never   rarely   sometimes   usually   always

Do you feel good about the clothes you wear to school?
never   rarely   sometimes   usually   always

Is the house that you live in kept clean?
never   rarely   sometimes   usually   always

Do your parents leave you home alone at night?
never   rarely   sometimes   usually   very often

Do your parents make you come home at a certain time at night?
never   rarely   sometimes   usually   always

Do your parents let you stay up as late as you want to watch television?
never   rarely   sometimes   usually   always

When you are going out, do your parents ask you where?
never   rarely   sometimes   usually   always

Do your parents allow you to smoke tobacco?
yes   no

Emotional Abuse

Do your parents ever scream or yell at you?
your mother: never   rarely   sometimes   often
your father: never   rarely   sometimes   often

Do your parents ever call you names or curse you?
your mother: never   rarely   sometimes   often
your father: never   rarely   sometimes   often

Do you feel like you can talk to your parents about problems you have?
your mother: never   rarely   sometimes   often
your father: never   rarely   sometimes   often

Do your parents ever say things to hurt your feelings?
your mother: never   rarely   sometimes   often
your father: never   rarely   sometimes   often

Does it ever seem like your parents are better to your brother(s) and/or
        sister(s) than they are to you?
your mother: never   rarely   sometimes   often
your father: never   rarely   sometimes   often

Do your parents ignore you when you want to talk to them?
your mother: never   rarely   sometimes   often

your father: never   rarely   sometimes   often

Physical Abuse

Do your parents spank you?
your mother: never   rarely   sometimes   often
your father: never   rarely   sometimes   often

If your mother spanks you, she most often uses:
      her hand   belt
      switch   paddle
      other: explain

If your father spanks you, he most often uses:
      his hand   belt
      switch   paddle
      other: explain

Do your parents ever strike you, other than spanking, with their fist, foot, or
      other object?
your mother: never   rarely   sometimes   often
your father: never   rarely   sometimes   often

As a result of your parents punishing you, have you ever received bruises or
      other injuries?

your mother:	never	once
	two or three times	more than three times
your father:	never	once
	two or three times	more than three times

Have you ever had to go to a doctor as a result of your parents punishing
      you?
your mother: never   once   more than once
your father: never   once   more than once

      The second example (Brown, 1975) is a scale designed to measure
the respondent's perception of the police role in terms of service versus
crime fighting tasks. When the following coding scheme is applied to
positively stated service role items and negatively stated crime role items,
the higher scores reflect a service orientation while lower scores reflect a
crime fighter orientation.

Very Strongly Agree	Strongly Agree	Agree	Disagree	Strongly Disagree	Very Strongly Disagree

This is then reversed for negatively stated service role items and positively stated crime role items.

POLICE ROLE PERCEPTION SCALE

1. A police officer should help out an ex-offender to keep him from getting into trouble again.
2. Police should enforce the law and nothing more.
3. The police should provide personal and community services of a non-criminal and non-emergency nature.
4. The police do not have time for services of a non-criminal nature.
5. The police should refer a person requesting assistance to the appropriate agency if they cannot help.
6. Services to the public are an essential part of the police job.
7. Police officers should spend most of their time providing services to the community.
8. The best reason for a police officer to attend school is to learn new ways to apprehend suspects.
9. The police should maintain contact with other criminal justice agencies only if it will aid them in apprehending offenders.
10. Major disasters should be dealt with by agencies other than the police.
11. Police officers should take it upon themselves to give directions to out-of-town motorists who appear to be lost.
12. The best police policy would be to answer only calls that report a violation of the law.
13. The police are in an excellent position to educate our citizenry in understanding of the law.
14. It is logical that the police should handle all types of traffic problems.
15. Too many police officers are obsessed with criminal investigations.
16. The police should provide information, instruction, and consultation to various citizen's groups.
17. There is much more to being a police officer than enforcing the law.

18. Helping a motorist with a stalled car should not be considered part of a police officer's duty.
19. Giving advice to citizens is not an important police function.
20. Besides apprehending criminals, there are many things equally or more important that the police should do for their community.
21. Combating crime should be considered the most fundamental aspect of police work.
22. Police work should concentrate more on the enforcement of the criminal law than it currently does.
23. Most police departments do not provide enough services to their communities.
24. Crime is the heart of the police problem.
25. Most communities need the police to spend more of their time protecting the community from crime.
26. There is little need for a police officer to approach people in the line of duty unless he is suspicious of criminal activity.

The next instrument (Gottfredson, 1970) also employs a Likert scoring scheme, but elicits responses to a series of vignettes that are designed to measure attitudes toward juvenile detention. These attitudes are likely to serve as dependent variables with hypotheses that they are effected, for example, by the age, education, socioeconomic status or other characteristics of the respondents. Note that the numerical scores for a scale can always be reversed. They are not provided for the scale below. The researcher can therefore code *certainly not detain* lowest and *certainly detain* as highest or reverse that coding scheme. It would be a good idea to look ahead to your analysis and determine which direction of coding would be most readily interpretable. For example, suppose you hypothesize that the role perceptions of police officers as measured in the above scale are correlated with their attitudes toward juvenile detention as measured in the Gottfredson scale below. Further assume that the specific direction of your research (alternative) hypothesis is that those whose role scores reflect a service orientation will tend to less frequently advocate juvenile detention, while those with more of the crime fighter orientation will tend to favor juvenile detention. Your results would probably be most readily interpretable if a positive correlation was consistent with your research hypothesis. Therefore, high scores on the *Police Role Perception* scale should correspond with high scores on the *Attitudes Toward Juvenile Detention*.

Given the scoring scheme for the role perception scale delineated above (higher scores reflecting a service orientation), it is necessary to code the *certainly not detain* items high and *certainly detain* items low so that a positive correlation would be yielded if respondents favoring detention (low) tend to have crime fighter orientations (also low), while those less favorably disposed to detention (high scores) are also inclined to score service (high) orientations. However, it may be confusing to score those favoring detention as low, but if this is reversed so that those favoring detention are scored high, then it is necessary to either (1) reverse scoring on the role scale so that high scores reflect the crime fighter role or (2) to recognize that a negative correlation would then be consistent with the research hypothesis. The former may be most desirable. If you scored the detention scale so that *certainly not detain* is equal to zero and *certainly detain* equals five, then the role scale would simply be reversed so that positively stated service role items are scored zero for *very strongly agree* and five for *very strongly disagree*. However, remember that there is no right or wrong coding scheme. What is essential is that it is properly interpreted at the analytical stage and this is facilitated by looking ahead to your analysis during the design of the coding scheme.

ATTITUDES TOWARD JUVENILE DETENTION SCALE

Instructions: Twenty-five case situations or vignettes requiring detention decisions are presented in this questionnaire. The vignettes portray relatively complex family situations, but most persons whose work involves juvenile detention decisions will discover much that is familiar in the problems presented.

Please read each of the vignettes. In each case, six choices are open to you. Please check only one choice for each vignette.

1. Ernie, age 17, is brought in by the police charged with assault with a deadly weapon. According to the officers, he and two friends crashed a party, disrupted the proceedings by bullying, and made insulting advances toward the girls. In the ensuing fight, Ernie used a broken coke bottle to seriously gash the host's arm.

Contrary to witnesses' statements, Ernie insists that he was invited to the party and did nothing objectionable there. He justifies use of the weapon in that five or six of the boys jumped him because he was making out with the girls.

A Central Records check reveals several police contacts, at least one year old, due to suspicious loitering and curfew violation. Eight months ago, he and the same two friends were placed on probation after they stole a car to drive to a party. Progress reports indicate very satisfactory improvement. He has avoided further difficulty, has re-enrolled in school, and has maintained passing grades while working part time in a gas station.

Certainly not detain	Probably not detain	Slightly against detention	Slightly for detention	Probably detain	Certainly detain

2.   Sally, age 14, is brought in by her parents, who insist she be detained. They describe her as becoming increasingly defiant, disobedient, poor in her schoolwork, and truant. They say the trouble started when she met Tina, a 16-year-old dropout who "does as she pleases."

Recently, Sally stayed out overnight on a weekend, without permission. Earlier in the day, she and Tina had been picked up as runaways after two days away from home, apparently heading for New York. The parents suspect the girls of sexual misbehavior and drug use.

Sally admits trying to get away from her parents by going to live in New York with relatives. She denies the other allegations and describes her father's temper and parents' arguments as intolerable. She states also she probably will run away again if the parents' contemplated divorce becomes a reality.

Certainly not detain	Probably not detain	Slightly against detention	Slightly for detention	Probably detain	Certainly detain

3.   Ronnie, age 13, is carried in by two policemen, kicking and screaming. They report that a variety shop owner and his wife had caught the boy who had, six times in the past month, dashed into the store and run off with small items. His description had been given to the police, and it corresponded with that which had been given by other petty theft victims in the area. The boy would not give his name; however, a customer at the shop identified him and accused him of minor acts of mischief in the neighborhood.

The school vice-principal reveals that Ronnie was enrolled eight weeks ago, from out-of-state, and expelled four weeks later due to fights, defiance, and disobedience. He has not been back, and the family has not responded.

A telephone call to the home elicits from the boy's aunt that his mother, who is at work, has not been told of his difficulties. The aunt states that she doesn't want to worry her. The mother was recently widowed and had to move to the city to support her children. The mother, by phone, verified the aunt's statements and said she would come to the office immediately.

Certainly not detain	Probably not detain	Slightly against detention	Slightly for detention	Probably detain	Certainly detain

4.   Bill, a 17-year-old college freshman, is brought in by police when neighbors complained of a wild party. Police found six people, under age 21, in various stages of undress and obvious intoxication. Alcoholic beverages and marijuana cigarettes were found in the apartment. Bill is the youngest of the six.

From the information the police have put together, it is apparent that Bill has been living for several weeks with the 19-year-old coed to whom the apartment is rented. Particles of marijuana were found in his shirt pocket. He has no police record.

Bill states that he has never been in trouble, says he has been living with the girl, admits he was a little high from drinking, but claims he has never used marijuana. His claim that he carried marijuana cigarettes for his girlfriend is supported by her statement to the police. The father, on the phone, states, "Ship him back here, or do what you like. He insisted on going to school out there. He got himself into trouble, now he'll have to face it like a man."

Certainly not detain	Probably not detain	Slightly against detention	Slightly for detention	Probably detain	Certainly detain

5.   Phillip, age 17, the son of a prominent doctor, is brought in, charged with vehicular hit and run, while driving well over the speed limit, according to witnesses. His car allegedly sideswiped another when he failed to stop at a red light. An estimated $300 damage was done to the other vehicle, and the driver suffered slight injuries.

It is established that Phillip, an only child, had his license revoked two weeks ago, for one year, due to repeated moving violations. He has had several police contacts in the past three years for illegal use of firearms, being intoxicated, participating in wild parties, reckless driving, and possession of alcohol. However, no court action was taken in any of these situations. His school record is above average, and he is known as a good boy, but wild. The parents are very cooperative with the authorities, but they are ineffectual in controlling Phillip's behavior.

Certainly not detain	Probably not detain	Slightly against detention	Slightly for detention	Probably detain	Certainly detain

6.   Linda, age 17, a reported runaway, was found living with her 24-year-old fiancee. She admits she has been with him two weeks and is two months pregnant. For the past four months, her parents have refused them permission to marry. When she discovered her pregnancy, she decided to leave home because she was afraid of her parents' reaction.

Linda has no police record, and she appears average in all respects. However, her parents insist that she be "locked up." They feel she would be a bad influence on the younger children and do not want her "contaminating the rest of the family with her filth."

School officials state Linda has average grades in her senior year. She could be reinstated; and if the lost work were made up, she could be graduated with her class in three months.

Certainly not detain	Probably not detain	Slightly against detention	Slightly for detention	Probably detain	Certainly detain

7.   Robert, age 14, is brought in after a neighbor discovered him in an act of intercourse with her 10-year-old daughter. He ran, and the woman states she obtained the following information from her daughter while the police were looking for him. Robert forced her the first time, then threatened to tell her father if she didn't keep doing it. Repeated sex acts have occurred in the past several months, with both the 10-year-old and her 11-year-old sister. The sister, under questioning, gave the same story and indicated that Robert had similarly coerced her 11-year-old girlfriend.

Robert's mother, when contacted by the police regarding his whereabouts, was moderately intoxicated, sexually provocative, and relatively unconcerned about her son. The father is a traveling salesman who is currently on the road.

Robert is sullen and uncommunicative, saying only that he didn't do anything wrong; he sees his parents doing it all the time. He has no police record. The school states that he is one and one-half years retarded academically; except for several unexcused absences, his school adjustment is described as satisfactory.

Certainly not detain	Probably not detain	Slightly against detention	Slightly for detention	Probably detain	Certainly detain

8. Danny, an hour ago, struck a male teacher with his fist, threatened to break a chair over his head, then walked out of the school. After this happened, three students reported that he repeatedly struck them and threatened them with beatings if they told on him. The high school vice principal requests that a petition be filed on Danny, and asks that he be detained due to his propensity for physical attacks on others.

A month ago he verbally threatened two teachers. During the resultant parent conference, the mother confided that she was afraid of him because he had struck her and his step-father on several occasions. She felt that the severe beatings the step-father had administered when Danny was younger had turned the boy into a bully. Though bright, he has been an underachiever academically. He has no police record.

Certainly not detain	Probably not detain	Slightly against detention	Slightly for detention	Probably detain	Certainly detain

9. Sam, age 14, stole a horse. His father had always promised him one, and a year ago he had been given one by his father's friend. However, the feed bill accumulated and the father did not want the expense. He sold the horse for a few dollars more than the bill. Several times Sam asked the father's permission to ride the horse, but he was refused. Yesterday morning he took the horse and rode 15 miles to a friend's ranch where he had stayed often for several days.

The farmer is pressing charges for grand theft. The father is furious at the boy's actions and wants him punished. Sam has no police record, but his school record is very poor. He has several failing grades, poor study habits, and has been absent any time he could manage it. His only interests are animals and ranching.

Certainly not detain	Probably not detain	Slightly against detention	Slightly for detention	Probably detain	Certainly detain

10.   Joe, age 17, has been in trouble since age 11 for petty theft, grand theft (auto), truancy, intoxication, receiving and selling stolen goods, and neighborhood gang fights. He spent eleven months in a boys' rehabilitation center, where he made a very good adjustment; and he has been home four months. Reports indicate his progress since returning to the community is well above average. He has worked steadily as a mechanic's helper, has given part of his salary to his family, and his employer has only praise for him.

However, parents of a 15-year-old girl insist that he be locked up. They claim he raped their daughter by getting her drunk and taking advantage of her. Joe admits to the sexual intimacy, but he states that they love each other, want to get married, and "one thing led to another." He feels that her parents were against him from the beginning because of his record, and they are trying to get rid of him by having him put in jail.

Certainly not detain	Probably not detain	Slightly against detention	Slightly for detention	Probably detain	Certainly detain

11.   Barbara, age 15, is due to be released from medical observation this afternoon. She attempted suicide, two days ago, by an overdose of barbiturates obtained outside the home. In an interview this morning she revealed that she has been on pills and pot for almost six months. A boy she has been dating has kept her supplied, and she recently "went all the way with him." She feels that her life is ruined, that she would be better off dead, and states "they should have left me alone."

Barbara's mother has noticed her daughter "acting strangely lately," but states her daughter would not confide in her. Barbara has been staying out late at night and had to be disciplined. School officials report that Barbara was an outstanding student, but they state her work has deteriorated this year.

Certainly not detain	Probably not detain	Slightly against detention	Slightly for detention	Probably detain	Certainly detain

12.   Pete is brought in today by police, along with four companions, after they were discovered in a stolen car. Pete was not driving and claims ignorance that the car was "hot." Pete is 15.

A court hearing is pending on a petition alleging that he is guilty of grand theft (auto) and $1,000 property damage to the stolen vehicle (plus several parked cars) while trying to elude the police during a high-speed chase.

However, two of the boys confessed to the police that they stole the car. They state that when Pete was told about it, he said "Crazy man, these are the wheels we need for the party tonight."

The school authorities describe Pete as an indifferent student who associates with the "undesirable element." They say he is usually found wherever there is trouble. The parents both work; and though they seem to mean well, they do not take any definite action about Pete's behavior.

Certainly not detain	Probably not detain	Slightly against detention	Slightly for detention	Probably detain	Certainly detain

13.   Ted, age 16, has been known to the Probation Department for the past five years. At first, it was petty theft and malicious mischief. Then it was bicycle and auto theft for the sale of parts. He has been to rehabilitation facilities twice, and he is still on probation.

Last night, he was picked up at his home after investigation revealed that he had several younger boys working for him stripping cars. He acted as a fence for the stolen goods, giving the boys a small percentage of the selling price. The police have statements from most of the boys, and they found a quantity of stolen goods in the garage at Ted's residence. He denies everything, says he's being "framed," and demands an attorney.

Ted's parents died when he was seven and he has lived with various relatives ever since. He currently lives with an uncle who appears unconcerned about the boy's actions. Ted is not in school, nor is he employed.

Certainly not detain	Probably not detain	Slightly against detention	Slightly for detention	Probably detain	Certainly detain

14.   Martin, age 17, is vaguely aware of his surroundings. He was medically examined and found to be under the influence of marijuana. Five marijuana cigarettes were found on his person by the police when they arrived at his friend's house after being summoned by the latter's parents.

Martin returned to the community two days ago after seven months in a Youth Authority facility. The commitment was the result of his conviction for the possession and sale of narcotics. The boy's father is currently in prison on the same charge. The mother has no influece on her older children other than to engender guilt after they do something wrong.

Certainly not detain	Probably not detain	Slightly against detention	Slightly for detention	Probably detain	Certainly detain

15.   Sharon, age 13, is charged with repeated shoplifting. The police request that she be detained. The store manager stated that this was the second time she had been caught in his store, and he gave the names of three other store managers who had similar experiences with her. A check of local merchants turned up nine known instances of shoplifting in seven stores. They have been previously unwilling to prosecute because she seemed like such a nice girl.

A school counselor reports that Sharon, an only child, is a quiet girl of average ability who has been no problem in school. The principal states that both parents have good jobs; they are described by teachers as "rather strange, aloof, uncommunicative people."

Sharon indicates that she knows she was wrong in what she did, but she "likes to have nice things like other girls," and her parents claim they are "too poor to waste money" on the things she asks for. These are the same statements Sharon made to each shopkeeper after being caught stealing.

Certainly not detain	Probably not detain	Slightly against detention	Slightly for detention	Probably detain	Certainly detain

16.   John, age 14, has been increasingly truant during his last year in junior high school. When picked up at his home by the attendance officer, John insisted that he would not return to school.

Both parents work, but they have escorted him to school daily. As soon as they are out of sight, he returns home to watch television. They report that he behaves reasonably at home, but he only wants to watch TV, which he seems to be content to do for days at a time. They complain that they have tried everything, including harsh discipline, and now are at their wits' end.

John states that he hates school, sees no reason to go. "The teachers are stupid, and the subjects are more so." He claims to have no problem with the work, when he wants to do it. This is supported by the school report which indicates that he has a superior IQ, but is failing all subjects due to 30 days' absence out of the last 60.

Certainly not detain	Probably not detain	Slightly against detention	Slightly for detention	Probably detain	Certainly detain

17.   Henry, age 12, has repeatedly been the subject of angry phone calls to the police due to damage he has allegedly done with stones and bricks. To date, he has been accused of breaking three school windows, a store window, and windows in two neighboring homes. He has also inflicted minor injuries upon other children. Today, police report he threw a stone through the windshield of a passing police car.

His statement is, "they make me mad, and I throw rocks," and he childishly justifies his actions. A neighbor asserts also that the boy turned on a hose down his chimney after he wet him while putting out a fire the boy had set on the man's property.

The school describes Henry as a very poor student who has little ability and a very nasty temper. He comes from a transient family of marginal means. The father is suspected of alcoholism.

Certainly not detain	Probably not detain	Slightly against detention	Slightly for detention	Probably detain	Certainly detain

18.   Teresa, age 15, on probation for petty theft, is the subject of a complaint filed by her aunt, who states "I went to see my sister, but just Teresa and three boys were in the house. She was having sex with all of them at one time, in different ways. From what I've been able to find out, she is sleeping with every boy in the neighborhood. Sometimes she gets

money for it. From the way they act, I think she has had sex with her older brothers, too. My sister is an alcoholic and can't take care of the children. She made a very bad marriage after Teresa's father died. I want Teresa to live with me."

Teresa is silent, except for one angry outburst: "That bitch, what does she care what I do. Nobody did anything when my stepfather raped me. He likes me better than my mother."

The vice-principal describes her as a very indifferent student who is considered both crazy and "fast." Boys continually flock around her.

Certainly not detain	Probably not detain	Slightly against detention	Slightly for detention	Probably detain	Certainly detain

19.   Audrey, a 13-year-old girl, was referred by the police for running away from home and being incorrigible. Audrey had left home and was staying at her maternal grandmother's house. Mr. Marens, her father, had reported her as a runaway because he didn't want her at the grandmother's. Since Audrey's natural mother had died there was a lot of hostility between Mr. Marens and the maternal grandmother. Mr. Marens stated that the grandmother was not able to properly supervise the child. Audrey's reason for moving to her grandmother's was that she just couldn't get along with her stepmother. She hated her since she had moved in soon after her mother died. Audrey stated that she was always wrong and her stepmother was always right. She refused to return to her father's home and insisted that she be granted permission to stay with her grandmother. The father has legal custody.

Certainly not detain	Probably not detain	Slightly against detention	Slightly for detention	Probably detain	Certainly detain

20.   Rudy is a 16-year-old boy referred by the police for auto theft. He was apprehended after the police chased a 1965 Ford which had been reported stolen. The youngster stopped the car and was walking away when the police caught up with him. He denied being the one driving the car and when brought into the juvenile office he stated he knew his rights and wanted an attorney. He strongly denied stealing the car and challenged the officers to prove it.

He stated that he wasn't in the car when apprehended. Rudy insisted that nobody was going to railroad him into admitting it and that he had been that route before. He refused to answer any further questions.

Certainly not detain	Probably not detain	Slightly against detention	Slightly for detention	Probably detain	Certainly detain

21.   Alvin, 15, was referred to the probation department by police. He was arrested at home on information supplied by two other young adults who implicated Alvin in burglary of seven rifles from Ace Gun Shop. The two young adults are free on bond of $1,000 each, and they turned over to police five rifles. They and Alvin are members of the "Last Chance" gang. Alvin is alleged to have the other two weapons.

Alvin seems marginally retarded but this has not been determined. He told investigating officers that he had no guns, had not pulled a job, and as far as he is concerned, "the cops can go to hell." His father and mother accompanied Alvin to the probation department, were very defensive of their son and stated that authorities "have nothing to go on" in making this arrest. They have no guns in their house according to them and insist that Alvin is a "good boy."

Throughout this time, Alvin sat with a sneer on his face and refused to talk with police except to say that "Maybe I'll get me a lawyer."

Certainly not detain	Probably not detain	Slightly against detention	Slightly for detention	Probably detain	Certainly detain

22.   Richard is a 16-year-old boy who was referred by the police for theft over $50. The youngster was apprehended breaking into a 1967 Oldsmobile in a shopping center. Richard admitted that he and three of his friends has been breaking into cars for several months and stealing credit cards from the autos. The police determined that the boys had taken about 100 credit cards. The cards were being sold by them to youngsters at the high school for $2 each. Merchandise and gasoline were being charged against the credit cards in the amount of $4,500.

During the investigation, Richard's attitude was one of arrogance and defiance. He stated he had notified his father already and that his father and his attorney were on the way to pick him up. Mr. Smith is a well-known businessman here in the city. Richard said his father would make complete restitution, and he couldn't understand what all the fuss was about.

Mr. Smith and his attorney arrived, and they wanted the child released immediately. Mr. Smith stated he would make complete restitution to cover all losses.

Certainly not detain	Probably not detain	Slightly against detention	Slightly for detention	Probably detain	Certainly detain

23.   Max is a 12-year-old youngster referred to the juvenile probation department by the police department for shoplifting a 59-cent belt from Ajax Department Store. His attitude regarding the referral is passive, and he states he has stolen better articles in the past. He asked to be locked up at the detention home because some of his friends were there. He was told that "they eat good" there and he wants to go see for himself.

Certainly not detain	Probably not detain	Slightly against detention	Slightly for detention	Probably detain	Certainly detain

24.   Jerry and Paul, brothers ages 10 and 11, were referred by the police for burglary and theft. Jerry and Paul were apprehended by the police while in a restaurant. They had broken into the place around midnight and were eating some food when arrested. They had also taken some milk, potato chips, and bread in a paper bag. They seemed frightened. They admitted to breaking into the cafe to get some food, as both were very hungry. When quetioned regarding the food they were preparing to take with them, they stated they were going to take it home to their brothers and sisters.

(Further investigation proved that there were nine children in the home. The father had been killed nine months previous to this incident and there was no food in the home.)

Certainly not detain	Probably not detain	Slightly against detention	Slightly for detention	Probably detain	Certainly detain

25. Tim, age 11, is accused by police of being one of three boys who broke into his school last weekend and turned it into a shambles. Supplies were scattered, ink and paints smeared on the walls, books torn, and teachers' desks broken open.

A stopwatch taken from one desk was found on Tim when he was taken into custody at his home. He admitted everything, and the father attempted to thrash him on the spot. Both parents insisted that the boy deserved to be severely punished "for the disgrace to our family."

Tim seems bewildered by his own actions. He says that they saw the open window, went in, got started, and couldn't stop. It was his idea to smear the paint and ink. There is no history of previous difficulty.

Certainly not detain	Probably not detain	Slightly against detention	Slightly for detention	Probably detain	Certainly detain

Interview Schedules

Though not used as widely as the questionnaire, there are some excellent interview schedules available for collecting data in criminal justice. Probably the most widely known are those used in the victimization surveys conducted under the auspices of the National Crime Survey (NCS) program. Numerous critiques of official crime data have revealed both reliability and validity problems with official crime data (*e.g.,* see Nettler, 1978). Consequently, the Bureau of the Census has been charged with the collection of crime data by interviewing representative samples of citizens regarding their experiences as victims of crime. Below is a segment of the NCS interview schedule that is employed for the interview of individuals regarding the perpetration of crimes against them.

INDIVIDUAL SCREEN QUESTIONS

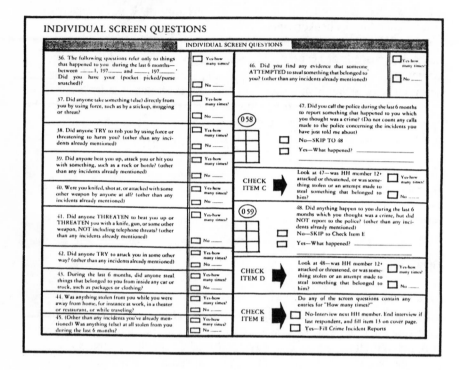

Source: Wesley G. Skogan *Issues in the Measurement of Victimization*
Washington, D.C.: U.S. Department of Justice, 1981, pp. 8.

The second example of an interview schedule was developed and used by one of the authors in the evaluation of a community project designed to impact upon youthful drinking and driving. This particular instrument was intended to measure adult perceptions of the problem, while a questionnaire was administered to a sample of youth to measure their behavior and perceptions. Note that the interview schedule is structured to facilitate a conversational flow from one question to the next. A pre-coded answer sheet should be completed for each respondent to facilitate keypunching or data entry at a terminal.

Read: Good (morning/afternoon/evening), my name is _____.
We are conducting a survey for the Washington County Youth Alcohol
Highway Safety Pilot Project.
Read: This number has been chosen at random for participation in the
survey. Is this a personal residence?

( ) Yes ( ) No

We are sorry to have bothered you. Thank you for your time.
Read: May I speak with someone present now in the household who is 19
years of age or older, and willing to participate in the survey?

( ) Yes ( ) No

We are sorry to have bothered you. Thank you for your time.
Read: I would like to ask you a few questions. Your responses will be very
valuable and will remain strictly confidential. They will be used for statistical
purposes only. If you object to a particular question, you, of course, may
refuse to answer it.
Read: There are many problems and social issues facing our country at this
time. I'd like to know how important you feel some of them are.

1a. How important a problem is crime in Washington County?
            Extremely important   (1)
            Very important   (2)
            Somewhat important   (3)
            Not at all   (4)

1b. How important a problem do you think drug abuse is in
      Washington County?
            Extremely important   (1)
            Very important   (2)
            Somewhat important   (3)
            Not at all   (4)

1c. How important a problem is drunk driving in Washington
      County?
            Extremely important   (1)
            Very important   (2)
            Somewhat important   (3)
            Not at all   (4)

1d. How important a problem is drinking and driving by
      teenagers?
            Extremely important   (1)
            Very important   (2)

Somewhat important	(3)
Not at all	(4)

Read: I'm going to read you a series of statements describing some aspect surrounding the use of alcoholic beverages by teenagers. You are to indicate if you strongly agree, somewhat agree, or strongly disagree or somewhat disagree with each statement.

2a.   Alcohol use among the teenagers (ages 13-18) in Washington
County is a problem in our community.

Strongly agree	(1)
Somewhat agree	(2)
Somewhat disagree	(3)
Strongly disagree	(4)

2b.   Drinking alcoholic beverages in moderation is acceptable
for teenagers ages 15-18.

Strongly agree	(1)
Somewhat agree	(2)
Somewhat disagree	(3)
Strongly disagree	(4)

2c.   Highway accidents and fatalities in our community could be
reduced if alcohol use by teenagers was lessened.

Strongly agree	(1)
Somewhat agree	(2)
Somewhat disagree	(3)
Strongly disagree	(4)

2d.   Education about alcohol use and abuse is a waste of time
and energy.

Strongly agree	(1)
Somewhat agree	(2)
Somewhat disagree	(3)
Strongly disagree	(4)

Read: What should happen to teenagers who are caught drinking and driving? *(Do not read the items. Circle appropriate items if mentioned in the subject's response.)*

Responses to Question 3.

Punishment left to parents	(1)
Should be jailed	(2)
Should be fined	(3)
License suspended	(4)
Required to do community services	(5)
Corporal punishment	(6)
Referral to educational program or DWI school	(7)
Nothing can be done	(8)
Don't know	(9)
Referral to alcohol treatment	(10)
Other	(11)

Read: Would you, as a citizen, support each of the following actions if proposed by public officials? Answer yes or no.

(1) Yes   (2) No   (3) Don't Know

4a. A large scale information and education
campaign on youthful drinking and driving.   (1) (2) (3)

4b. Education for high school students about
alcohol abuse and drunk driving.   (1) (2) (3)

4c. Youth involvement in efforts to prevent
drunk driving.   (1) (2) (3)

4d. Education program for teenagers arrested
for drinking violations.   (1) (2) (3)

4e. Greater police enforcement of laws
against teenage drinking.   (1) (2) (3)

4f. Greater police enforcement of laws
against sales of alcoholic beverages to minors.   (1) (2) (3)

4g. Swift, sure punishment of teenagers who violate
drinking laws.   (1) (2) (3)

5.   What do you think are the chances out of 100 that the police
would catch a teenager driving home after having three or
four alcoholic drinks? _____

6.   What do you think are the chances out of 100 that the police
would catch a teenager riding in a car and drinking
alcoholic beverages with friends for several hours? _____

7.   What do you think are the chances that a teenager driving 20 mph
above the speed limit would be caught? _____

8. If the police caught a teenager drinking and driving, what do you
    think are the chances out of 100 that each of the following
    would happen?
    a. They would be given a warning? _____
    b. They would be fined? _____
    c. They would have to attend DWI
       school? _____
    d. They would be placed on probation
       for at least a year? _____

Read: Finally, a few questions for classification purposes.

9. What is your age?
10. Do you have children of your own?
            Yes   (1)   No   (2) *(If No, skip to #15)*
11. How many? _____
12. What are their ages? _____
13. What are their sex? _____
14. What school(s) do they attend? _____
15. How many years of school did you complete? _____
16a. On an average day, during what hours do you watch TV?
            (DO NOT READ LIST! CIRCLE RESPONSE GIVEN)
                6 AM - 8 AM   (1)
                8 AM - 5 PM   (2)
                5 PM - 8 PM   (3)
                8 PM -11 PM   (4)
                11 PM or later   (5)
                Don't watch TV   (6) (skip to question 17)
16b. What channel do you usually watch? _____
17a. On an average day, during what hours do you listen to the radio?
            (DO NOT READ LIST! CIRCLE RESPONSES GIVEN)
                6 AM - 9 AM   (1)
                9 AM - 5 PM   (2)
                5 PM - 7 PM   (3)
                7 PM - Midnight   (4)
                Midnight to 6 AM   (5)
                Don't listen to radio   (6) (skip to question 18)
17b. What station do you usually listen to?
18. What newspapers do you usually read at least once a week?
19a. Have you heard of the Youth Action Group and/or Project Star?
            Yes   (1)   No   (2)
19b. (If Yes) Do you recall what the letters STAR stand for or the

purpose of the project?

Thank you for your cooperation. If you have any questions about the Washington County Youth Alcohol Highway Safety Project, please call 928-6581.

Remember that interviewing is a time-consuming process. The above schedule, administered by telephone, required an average of 20 to 25 minutes for completion. Training of interviewers is also very important. Both the instrument and interview techniques should be thoroughly reviewed prior to initiating data collection.

Secondary Data

Electing to utilize secondary data allows the researcher to economize in terms of time and resource expenditure. You can easily access sets of data that go far beyond the scope of what you could collect on your own. For most topics in criminal justice you will be able to identify such data sets already collected by other researchers. The major problem with this approach is that the data have ordinarily been collected for purposes different than those you have in mind. Consequently, validity questions sometimes plague secondary data.

Three major examples of secondary data sources for criminal justice researchers are the Uniform Crime Reports, the National Crime Surveys and reports of the Bureau of the Census. Presented below is a small data set based upon an NCS sample of 26 cities that a number of researchers have used in conducting ecological analyses. Brown and Woolley (1985) reviewed a number of these studies and identified some problems that can arise with the use of such data. However, with adequate caution these data can be used to address many different research questions. The two UCR columns represent rates for rape and auto theft as reported in the UCRs, while the NCS columns present corresponding measures from that source. Density was calculated by dividing population by land area as both were reported by the U.S. Bureau of the Census (1973).

DATA SET FOR 26 CITIES

ID	City	UCR Rape [a]	Vict. Rape [b]	UCR Auto Theft [a]	Vict. Auto Theft [b]	Population	Density
1	Boston	376	2.0	17998	86.0	641053	13936
2	Buffalo	191	2.0	4495	30.0	462783	11205
3	Cincinnati	203	2.0	2625	25.0	452550	5794
4	Houston	557	3.0	12035	32.0	1232407	2840
5	Miami	86	1.0	2754	18.0	335075	9769
6	Milwaukee	175	2.0	5219	29.0	717124	7549
7	Minneapolis	236	4.0	4590	41.0	434381	7884
8	New Orleans	243	3.0	6352	32.0	593471	3011
9	Oakland	220	3.0	4746	36.0	361613	6772
10	Pittsburgh	274	2.0	6628	43.0	520167	9423
11	San Diego	173	2.0	4527	25.0	696566	2198
12	San Francisco	540	3.0	9339	38.0	715674	15764
13	Washington, D.C.	596	1.0	4713	15.0	756510	12321
14	Atlanta	268	2.4	4034	28.5	497024	3780
15	Baltimore	537	1.4	8938	35.0	905759	11568
16	Cleveland	428	2.0	19855	76.3	751046	9895
17	Dallas	585	2.0	6914	24.4	844189	3178
18	Denver	434	3.0	7088	44.4	514678	5406
19	Newark	312	1.4	6929	36.9	382377	16271
20	Portland	144	2.6	3737	33.9	381877	4286
21	St. Louis	498	1.4	11865	47.3	622236	10167
22	Chicago	1529	3.0	32295	36.0	3362825	15107
23	Detroit	818	3.0	20522	49.0	1511336	10952
24	Los Angeles	2205	2.0	33720	42.0	2816111	6073
25	New York	3271	1.0	75865	26.0	7894851	26343
26	Philadelphia	588	1.0	16040	42.0	1948609	15164

[a] Number of offenses
[b] Rate per 1000 population

These data are only a sample of the three data sources mentioned. As a person in the field of criminal justice, you should become thoroughly familiar with their content. You should also carefully search for other available secondary data while undertaking the literature review for your topic.

Test Instruments

A wide variety of test instruments exist that may be useful in your research. One example of a scale widely used in criminal justice research is the Authoritarian Personality (F) Scale (Adorno, Frenkel-Brunswick, Levinson and Sanford, 1950). The criminal justice literature is replete with theoretical speculation and research regarding the personality structure of police and other personnel staffing the system. Any number of hypotheses regarding criminal justice personnel might be generated, with the "authoritarian personality" serving as either an independent or dependent variable. Likewise, authoritarianism might serve as a useful concept in the examination of clients of the criminal justice system. For example, it might be hypothesized that certain categories of offenders display higher levels of authoritarianism or that among the general citizenry authoritarianism is in some manner related to attitudes toward the criminal justice system.

Another major personality test widely used by researchers in criminal justice is the Minnesota Multiphasic Personality Inventory (MMPI). This is a lengthy test designed to measure 26 different areas of personality. It is discussed in most psychology texts and is often used for screening prospective criminal justice personnel and classifying offenders.

Occasionally the researcher may find that he/she needs to develop a test instrument. This is particularly likely when evaluation research is being conducted. The following is an example of a brief test developed by one of the authors to measure changes in levels of knowledge about alcohol use.

KNOWLEDGE OF ALCOHOL TEST

1. Out of the 10 major causes of death, how many are alcohol related?
   _____ 2
   _____ 3
   _____ 5
   _____ 8

2. Which of the following human functions is likely to be affected
      first by alcohol intake?
      _____ muscular coordination
      _____ judgement
      _____ speech
      _____ balance

3. Twelve ounces of beer, 5 ounces of wine, and 1 1/2 ounces of
      whiskey all contain:
      _____ different kinds of alcohol
      _____ about the same amount of alcohol
      _____ 40% alcohol
      _____ different amounts of alcohol

4. On an average weekend evening, how many drivers are drunk?
      _____ one out of every 10
      _____ one out of every 25
      _____ one out of every 50
      _____ one out of every 100

5. Alcohol is a factor in approximately what percentage of fatal
    automobile crashes?

    _____ 25%
    _____ 30%
    _____ 40%
    _____ 50%

6. Alcohol is a substance:

    _____ used at least occasionally by over 75% of all teenagers
    _____ that is abused more frequently than all other drugs combined
    _____ so toxic to humans that it causes diseases affecting many
            body systems
    _____ all of the above

7. Which of the following are ways to sober up a person? (Check one
    or more)

    _____ black coffee
    _____ waiting as long as necessary
    _____ exercise
    _____ a cold shower

8. Out of 2,000 drunk drivers how many are actually arrested?

    _____ 1
    _____ 10
    _____ 25
    _____ 50

9. Which of the following influences the effect of alcohol?

    _____ the amount of food in the stomach
    _____ the body weight of the individual
    _____ the time of day the alcohol is consumed
    _____ A and B only

10. What does "blood alcohol concentration" (BAC) mean?

    _____ percentage of alcohol in a person's bloodstream
    _____ ounces of alcohol that a person has consumed in a given
            time period
    _____ the level of alcohol in the blood which causes drunkeness
    _____ all of the above

11. During the ten year period of the Vietnam War, America lost
    approximately 55,000 men. How many lives were lost due to alcohol
    related car accidents during that same ten year period?

_____ 55,000
_____ 100,000
_____ 200,000
_____ 275,000

12. How much more likely is it that you'll have an accident if your "Blood Alcohol Concentration" (BAC) level is 0.15 than when you are sober?

_____ 5 times greater chance
_____ 10 times greater chance
_____ 15 times greater chance
_____ 25 times greater chance

Putting the Instrument Together

An effective data collection instrument must be carefully prepared. This requires a great deal of thought and time. Moreover, preparation for data collection does not end with a completed instrument. Once developed, the instrument must be pretested at least once with an appropriate sample. Quality control procedures must then be planned for all stages of data collection. No matter how good the instrument appears, numerous problems can arise in the field that may bias the data.

The following outline provides helpful hints for review when constructing a questionnaire or interview schedule.

I. Decide on the following:
   A. Type of Instrument
      1. Questionnaire
      2. Interview Schedule
   B. Types of Questions to be Asked
      1. Direct questions that require a factual answer
      2. Perceptual questions that ask the respondent to provide their personal perception or attitude
   C. Nature of the Question
      1. Close-Ended
         a. multiple choice
         b. dichotomous
      2. Open-Ended

II. Decide what the question is to elicit:
   A. Facts such as the age, race, education and occupation of the respondents

   B. Perceptions and attitudes of the respondents, such as
      what they estimate as the probability of apprehension
      for a particular violation of the law
   C. Verification of other information or "lie scales"
   D. Knowledge, such as the penalties associated with law
      violations or constitutional rights of the accused

III. Avoid these problems when constructing questions:
   A. Ambiguous questions that cannot be understood
   B. Difficult questions or phraseology that respondents
      cannot understand
   C. Value-laden questions in which the researcher is
      providing cues such as "should" or "ought"
   D. Questions that are too lengthy
   E. Double-Barreled questions which are really two
      questions in one
   F. Questions that raise ethical issues such as the violation
      of subject's privacy

IV. Develop the flow of the instrument:
   A. Provide adequate instructions
   B. Begin with questions that are the least threatening
      and/or are easiest to answer
   C. Emphasize transitions
   D. Recheck for logical development

V. Validity and/or Reliability:
   A. Instruments should be pretested to assure that they
      work and consistently measure what they are
      supposed to
   B. Validity and reliability coefficients should be calculated
      and reported to establish the scientific merit of the
      instrument

Sampling

Once the data collection instrument is developed, the researcher must select a sample for the study. Sampling refers to the way that a representative group is drawn from a larger population. There are a variety of ways that this can be done. To insure valid data, it is important that some scientific procedures direct the way that cases are selected for the research. Random sampling is the most widely known technique. In a random sample each unit selected for study has an equal chance of selection with every other unit in the population. Therefore any spurious effect is evenly distributed over all cases and that effect is nullified. If this is so then the statistical findings related to the sample can be inferred to the population, with a small margin of error. The following are steps in the random sampling process.

A) Identify the population to be studied. (Let the circle symbolize the population.) Remember that a population must contain *all* the cases defined.

B) Let a portion of the population be extracted. This is a sample (smaller circles in Figure 3.1 labeled S1, S2, S3, etc.).

C) If your sample was drawn from the population so that each part of the population had an equal chance of being included in the sample, then it is said to be a *random sample.*

D) Within the limits of defined error (defined by statistical significance) each mean and each standard deviation of each should roughly approximate Mu and Sigma of the population.

E) Consequently, within the ever present error called *chance,* you can make inferences about the population from the statistics of the sample.

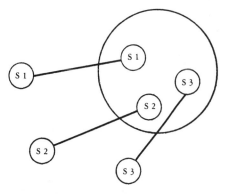

Figure 3.1 The Population and Samples

The most frequently used and possibly the least reliable method of sampling is Street Corner Sampling where a researcher goes out on the corner and asks anyone who comes along to answer questions. As there are so few controls, this procedure of selecting anyone on the street obviously yields little reliable information. For example, if a researcher were interested in surveying citizens regarding attitudes toward the police, different responses could be expected according to where they were located. We can expect for example that those attitudes vary by socioeconomic levels, age, race and/or sex. Therefore, biased measures may be the result of locating by a college campus, in a high income section of town, in an all-white neighborhood and so forth.

A correction to this street corner technique occurs when the researcher attempts to approximate the characteristics of the community by imposing strata on the persons that he or she asks to answer questions. To impose strata means that the researcher decides how many of what kind of persons he or she will include in the study. Typically these quotas are selected to reflect the demographic characteristics of the area. While this is an improvement, the study will still suffer since volunteers still introduce a bias into the sampling procedure.

Consequently, the social researcher is urged to avoid such sampling techniques except when there is absolutely no other way to gather the data. This might occur if the researcher were studying a special obscure population. In that case, a snowball sampling technique might be used. Snowball sampling occurs when an informant gives the researcher the names and addresses of other informants who are involved in the select population. For example, if the researcher wants to know the activity level of transvestites, he or she would have to find an active transvestite and ask for names of others who that person knows. Then the researcher finds the newly named transvestites and asks for further names. The longer the researcher follows this procedure, the larger the sample snowballs. The larger the sample, the greater the chance that the findings might be valid.

Random sampling can take many forms. If each person in a population has an equal chance of being selected, then the technique is called *simple random sampling*. If strata is imposed on a simple random sample, then the technique is called a *stratified random sample*. If national clusters of cities are studied it is called a *cluster random sample*.

Whichever form is used, the student needs to be aware that representativeness depends on scientific sampling. It is really worth the added time and effort to design a sampling technique that will guarantee valid interpretations to be made from the sample for the population.

Some students will notice from their examination of the literature that many of the sampling technqiues used by criminal justice researchers are questionable. For a variety of reasons, many criminal justice researchers have used samples of convenience rather than selecting subjects through more rigorous sampling techniques. Even so, the goal of science is to produce data that are representative of the population being studied. This can be accomplished only when some form of scientific sampling is designed into the study.

Exercises

1. Find three different data collection instruments from research reported in criminal justice journals. Describe each.

2. Develop a questionnaire that incorporates measures of independent, dependent and control variables.

3. Go to your library and locate each of the following sources of secondary data: Uniform Crime Reports, National Crime Surveys and Census Reports.

4. Locate research methodology texts and study different techniques of scientific sampling. Summarize three different methods. What are the advantages and disadvantages of each?

References

Adorno, T. W., Else Frenkel-Brunswik, D.J. Levinson, and R.N. Sanford *The Authoritarian Personality* (New York: Harper, 1950).

Brown, Stephen E. "Social Class, Child Maltreatment, and Delinquent Behavior" (1984) *Criminology* 22:259-278.

_____ Police Professionalism and Role Perception unpublished Master's Thesis, (1975) Eastern Kentucky University.

_____ and Thomas W. Woolley "The National Crime Survey Program: Problems in Sample Selection and Data Analysis" *Social Science Quarterly* (1985) 66:186-193.

Gottfredson, Donald *Measuring Attitudes Toward Juvenile Detention* (Davis, California: National Council on Crime and Delinquency, 1970).

Nettler, Gwynn *Explaining Crime* (2nd Edition) (New York: McGraw-Hill, 1978).

Skogan, Wesley G. *Issues in the Measurement of Victimization* (Washington, D.C.: U.S. Government Printing Office, 1981).

U.S. Bureau of the Census County and City Data Book, 1972
(Washington, D.C.: U.S. Government Printing Office, 1973).

4

Analyzing the Data

Statistical analysis represents one of the most important tools of the criminal justice researcher. Through the proper application of statistical tests, the data are analyzed and the findings are interpreted. Prior to a first course in research methods each student should have taken a course in statistics. While many students fear statistics because they are associated with the study of mathematics, their fears must not keep them from discovering how essential a tool statistics are for the social scientist. In fact, without the models and applications from statistics very little research could be accomplished. While a criminal justice researcher is not expected to be a sophisticated statistician, it is important to know when to refer to a statistician for help. In the interaction, it will be very important that the researcher understand the special language of statistics and the concepts that have been developed for data analysis. At a minimum the undergraduate student should understand the following statistical concepts.

1. The Normal Curve
2. Probability Theory
3. The Law of Large Numbers
4. Causal Relations
5. Levels of Measurement
6. Descriptive Statistics
7. Parametric and Nonparametric Statistics
8. Inferential Statistics

Each of these concepts is reviewed in this chapter. With an understanding of each of them, many of the most common errors of statistical design and analysis can be avoided.

The Normal Curve

Researchers use the normal curve as a model. It can be considered as an ideal type, something by which other things are measured. It is theoretical but it is assumed to exist at many places in nature and in the social world. Consider this simple example. If the UCR index crime rates for all American cities are plotted, the distribution should approximate the normal curve. This means that the crime rates of the various cities would be distributed around the mean in a known manner as depicted in Figure 4.1. About sixty-eight percent of all the measurements would fall within plus or minus one standard deviation from the mean, about ninety-five percent within plus or minus two standard deviations and so forth. In actual usage, the normal curve aids in making decisions about accepting or rejecting hypotheses. If some observation falls too great a distance from the mean of a group of measurements assumed to be normally distributed, one infers that this did not occur by chance alone. For example, one might conclude that cities with index crime rates more than two standard deviations away from the mean are actually lower or higher than the average. An understanding of probability theory is necessary to comprehend how inferences are drawn.

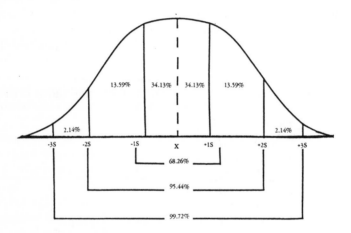

Figure 4.1 The Area Under the Normal Curve

Probability Theory

Many statistical tests are based on the assumption that the populations sampled are normally distributed. Other forms of sampling distributions can be assumed as well, but the logic underlying probability theory remains the same. Based on this assumption, distributions are compared and tested for differences. In some instances the test is a one-sample procedure involving the comparison of the mean (or some other parameter) of a single sample to some hypothesized value or standard derived from another source. Others are two-sample tests in which parameters derived from a pair of samples are contrasted. To illustrate probability theory with a one-sample test, suppose a police chief desires to test the proficiency of his/her officers in their handling of firearms. It is the chief's hope that the "average" officer's skills are at the "marksman" level or higher. A score of 75 percent on the Camp Perry Police Course is the minimum to qualify as marksman. So the chief's hope is that a representative sample of officers will score an average of 75 percent or better on that course. The null and research hypotheses in this case would be expressed as follows:

$$Ho: \mu \geq 75$$
$$Ha: \mu < 75$$

where:

μ = mean score of the sample
of officers
75 = required score for marksman
rating

In this example, a sample mean score of 75 percent or higher would support the null hypothesis. If the mean score was lower than 75 percent, it would be consistent with the research hypothesis. But how much lower must it be before one concludes that the sample score is in fact lower than the set standard? This will depend on the size of the critical region established by the researcher.

Several factors should be considered in establishing the size of the critical region (also referred to as the probability or significance level). Most important is the degree of error risk the researcher is willing to take. It is crucial to remember that the researcher *never proves* a hypothesis. Rather, he/she establishes a certain weight of evidence or probability. The following simple example is often used to illustrate the normal curve and probability theory. Suppose you wished to test a coin to determine if it was fair (*i.e.,* balanced). Thus, your null hypothesis would be that the coin is fair, while the research hypothesis would be that it is not. Common sense alone tells you that if you toss the coin ten times, keeping a record of the results and accumulate five heads and five tails, you would probably be satisfied that all is in order. However, suppose the result was six-four or four-six. What would you then conclude? What if you accumulated ratios of three-seven or seven-three; two-eight or eight-two? Clearly a fair coin will not necessarily accumulate five heads and five tails in ten trials. In fact, if you take a coin and begin plotting the results of trials of ten tosses you will find that the proportions of heads-tails in the series will approximate the normal curve as illustrated in Figure 4.2. Thus, the researcher must specify the ratio of heads-tails that would cast sufficient doubt on the null hypothesis to warrant its rejection. Yet the dilemma is that there is always some risk of falsely rejecting the null hypothesis (a Type I error). In this example, suppose the critical region was set to equal ratios of 10-0, 9-1, 8-2, 0-10, 1-9 and 2-8 (representing a two-tailed test). There would remain some risk that any one series of 10 tosses would yield results as extreme as these *even though the coin is fair,* this being a Type I error. But the Type II error is an inverse function of the Type I so that if the critical region is reduced, say to exclude the 8-2 and 2-8 ratios, the chances of failing to reject a false null hypothesis are increased assuming all else (*e.g.,* n) remains the same.

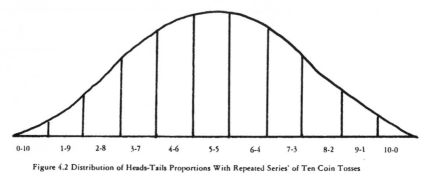

Figure 4.2 Distribution of Heads-Tails Proportions With Repeated Series' of Ten Coin Tosses

The Law of Large Numbers

Remember that much research is conducted by selecting a representative sample for analysis and drawing inferences or generalizations to the population. The normal curve (as well as other distributions) and probability theory are in effect when two important criteria are met. First, the sample must be generated randomly or through some scientific means before it is reasonable to assume that it accurately portrays the population from which it was drawn. Second, the sample n must be sufficiently large. In fact, the law of large numbers states that as the sample n increases, the sample mean ($\overline{X}$) more closely approximates the population mean (μ) and the standard deviation of the sample (S) more closely approximates the standard deviation of the population (σ). Consequently, estimates of popuation parameters improve as n is increased. This is illustrated in Figure 4.3. Ultimately then, the risk of both Type I and Type II errors are an inverse function of the sample n. However, there is a point of diminishing returns as n increases. Before undertaking a major research project, the topic of appropriate sample size should be studied. Kish (1965) is an excellent source for this topic.

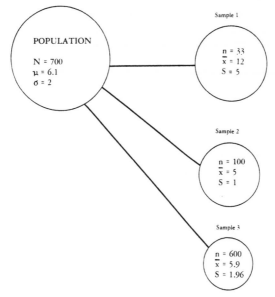

Figure 4.3 The Law of Large Numbers and Sample Size

Causal Relations

It is very difficult to establish causal relationships in social research. It is generally better to speak of the degree of association rather than causality unless specific methodological features are incorporated to assist the researcher in assessing causality. Statistical analysis is based on certain causal assumptions and does not address causal order per se. Very simply, the causal question is whether X really causes Y. Before one can conclude that this is the case, all rival hypotheses must be excluded. In the field of criminal justice many misconceptions have been the product of inadequate attention to causal issues. Some examples of situations where X and Y are closely associated, but obviously not cause and effect, will illustrate. The first example is the statistical association of ice cream consumption and the crime of rape. The two are positively associated (or correlated). That is, where ice cream consumption is higher, so is the frequency of the crime of rape. Yet it would be ludicrous to conclude that ice cream consumption *causes* rape. Clearly this is a spurious relationship that is a product of a third variable. Perhaps both phenomena are influenced by weather. Thus, in Figure 4.4, it is model b rather than a that accurately depicts the causal relations.

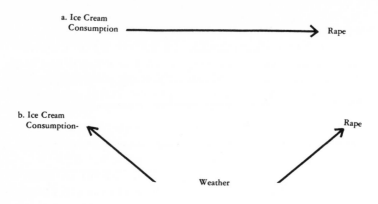

Figure 4.4 An Example of Rival Hypotheses and Spurious Associations

While this facetious example illustrates the point, it is not far removed from some examples of spurious conclusions that have been accepted in criminal justice. Consider the widespread belief that broken homes cause delinquent behavior among juveniles. It has repeatedly been found that the two are correlated, but recent research suggests that the correlation is a spurious product of a third factor, the quality of home relationships. As in the preceding example, the competing hypothesis is that broken homes and delinquency only appear to be related because both are dependent upon the quality of relationships in the home. Thus, when one controls for quality of relationships in the home, the presumed association between broken homes and delinquency vanishes as shown in Figure 4.5.

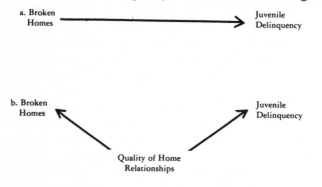

Figure 4.5 A Second Example of Rival Hypotheses and Spurious Associations

There are numerous possible explanations for any observed association, but unless specific methodological features to clarify causality are incorporated, a careful process of elaboration is necessary. Rosenberg's (1968) work is one of the classics addressing the elaboration process and should be consulted any time you are seeking to understand why and under what conditions categorically measured variables are associated.

Experiments and quasi-experimental designs are ideal for sorting out questions of causality. Experimental designs, in effect, control for all rival hypotheses by comparing equivalent groups before and after manipulation of the independent variable (*i.e.,* the treatment). In other words, because the two groups are assumed to be alike in all other respects, any differences after the experimental group is manipulated can be attributed to the treatment. Campbell and Stanley's (1966) classic work and the more recent book by Cook and Campbell (1979) should be consulted by the student desiring to understand these research designs. Unfortunately, experiments or even quasi-experiments can rarely be carried out in the field of criminal justice due to practical and ethical constraints. Consequently, criminal justice researchers have turned more and more to statistical techniques referred to as causal modeling, especially path analysis. While these techniques are helpful in assessing causal relations, they require relatively sophisticated understanding of statistics and are limited by the assumptions that they impose. Asher (1976) provides a good overview of these techniques.

Levels of Measurement

There are four levels of measurement ascribed to data. These are very important because they determine the techniques that can be employed in analyzing the data. The four levels of measurement are nominal, ordinal, interval and ratio.

Nominal
Nominal is the lowest level of measurement. At the nominal level all cases are assigned to different categories (or attributes) and counted according to their frequency of occurrence. Each case must be able to be assigned to one and only one category. Consequently, the categories are said to be exhaustive and mutually exclusive. The only distinction between the categories is that they are different. For example, twenty students in a criminal justice research class can be described in terms of the following variables measured at the nominal level:

Race: 15 whites, 5 blacks
Sex: 12 males, 8 females
Marital Status: 16 single, 4 married

These measures have no quantitative value and mathematical functions cannot be used to manipulate the data. Variables measured at the nominal level are inherently of that form. In other words, race for example, can only be measured as different categories. There simply is no other way to measure it. One of the most common inferential statistics assuming only nominal level data is chi square.

Ordinal

Ordinal data are grouped into ordered classes of categories (ranked from lowest to highest, etc.) as in social class being divided into lower, middle and upper. Another example is the ranks of police officers such as patrol officer, sergeant, lieutenant, captain. Note that these groupings imply differences without any defined magnitude between the categories. That is, there is no definition of the distance between categories. No mathematical functions can be used with ordinal level data. However, statistics based on ordinal measures do incorporate the concept of rank order in their calculations. An example is the gamma statistic.

Interval

Interval data, in addition to suggesting a rank order, have a fixed and constant distance between each of the points on the given dimension. If a zero is included in the scale, it is arbitrary and not an absolute zero. Temperature on a thermometer is an example of an interval scale as there are equidistant measurements, but no true zero. The absence of a true zero can be illustrated since there is never a case where there is no temperature. Another example of an interval scale is the Wechsler I.Q. score. While the scale is measured in equidistant intervals there is no possibility of a zero I.Q. as every person has some measurable intelligence on the Wechsler scales. Many criminal justice variables, including crime rates, can be measured at the interval level. Inferential statistics based on interval level data are quite different from those assuming only nominal or ordinal data because they can be mathematically manipulated in any way without losing their meaning. A simple test of whether data are interval level or higher is to ask whether an average that will be meaningful can be calculated. If so, the data are interval (or ratio). The correlation coefficient is one of the most basic statistics assuming interval or higher levels of measurement.

Ratio

Ratio level data has equal intervals and an absolute zero. For example, victimization survey data may yield values ranging from zero to any maximum frequency. Technically, the possibility of zero victimizations renders it ratio, but there is little practical distinction. Criminal justice researchers usually lump interval and ratio level measures together.

Keep in mind that the importance of the level of measurement is that it dictates the type of statistical analysis that can be employed. The higher the level of measurement, the more information there is contained in the data that can be incorporated in statistical formulae, and consequently, the more powerful the analysis becomes. A more powerful statistical test will increase the likelihood of detecting significant effects if they exist (*i.e.,* reduce the Type II error risk). For a detailed treatment of the important issue of statistical power, Cohen (1977) should be consulted. Interval or ratio level data can always be reduced to an ordinal level by collapsing categories should the need arise. However, data collected at the ordinal level can never be raised to a higher level because the information is not available. Thus, the general rule is to always collect data at the higher level. For example, in measuring age in a survey, respondents should be requested to record their actual age rather than checking a category. If the researcher needed age categories they could always be collapsed as desired at a later time. In sum, selecting the proper level(s) of measurement requires that the researcher look ahead to the statistical analysis that will be employed.

Descriptive Statistics

It is appropriate to use descriptive statistics whenever the researcher is studying a population or simply describing a sample (*i.e.,* treating a sample as a population). These statistics enable the researcher to characterize (*i.e.,* describe) a large set of data with a few measures. Descriptive statistics are often termed "univariate" because they are used to describe a single variable as opposed to reflecting relationships between varables. The most common descriptive statistics include measures of central tendency: the mean ($\overline{X}$), the median (Md) and the mode (Mo); measures of dispersion: the range (R), interquartile range (Q), variance (S^2) and standard deviation (S); and measures of frequency (frequency distributions).

Measures of Central Tendency

Measures of central tendency are intended to reflect the typical or average case in a distribution. The three most common measures of central tendency are the mean, median and mode. When a set of scores fall into a perfect normal curve, these three measures of central tendency will be identical as shown in Figure 4.6. However, this will rarely be the case with actual data sets and consequently, the researcher should be aware that a single measure of central tendency may be very misleading regarding the actual center of the distribution.

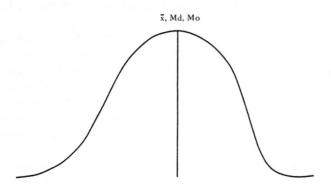

x̄, Md, Mo

Figure 4.6 Location of the Mean, Median, and Mode in a Normal Distribution

The mean ($\overline{X}$) of a distribution of numbers is the arithmetic average. The formula for the mean requires the researcher to take the sum (Σ) of a set of scores or cases and divide it by the total number of scores or cases (n).

$$\overline{X} = \frac{\Sigma X}{n}$$

As an example, consider the number of auto thefts reported per 1000 citizens in the 1973 National Crime Surveys for 13 selected cities. The mean for these data can be calculated as follows:

86
30
25          $\Sigma X = 450$
32            $n = 13$
18          $\Sigma X/n = 34.6$
29
41
32
36   The mean number of reported
43   auto theft victimizations per

25	1000 citizens in these 13
38	cities was 34.6.
_15_	
450	

Remember that it is impossible to take the mean of nominal or ordinal level data. The mean can be used only for measurements at the interval/ratio level.

The median is the score within a distribution above and below which half of the cases lie. It is a middle score that divides the distribution into two equal halves. In order to find the median, simply arrange the numbers from the lowest to the highest and count to the n + 1/2 position. The value of that position is the median. In the example used above, of the thirteen victimization rates when placed in numerical order, the median is the seventh position (32) as demonstrated below. When the n of cases is even, the median position will fall between two actual values so that it is necessary to average the two middle values to obtain the median. When n is an odd number a single case will fall at the median position.

15	1. Note that the cases are ordered
18	from lowest to highest
25	2. n + 1
25	13 + 1 = 14
29	3. n + 1/2
30	14/2 = 7
32	4. The median is the seventh
32	position (32). That position
36	has six values above and six
38	below it.
41	
43	
86	

Note that the median cannot be used with nominal level data because they cannot be ordered. It is generally the preferred measure of central tendency with ordinal data.

The mode is the most repeated number in a given distribution. It can be used with all levels of data, but is the only measure of central tendency that can be used with nominal data. The example of victimization rates is a bimodal distribution. That is, both 25 and 32 are modes. Figure 4.7 provides an illustration of a bimodal distribution.

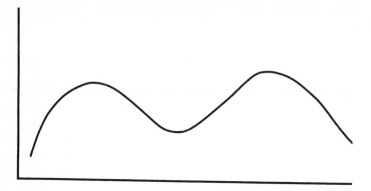

Figure 4.7 A Bimodal Distribution

We have seen that measures of central tendency are generally determined by the level of measurement. However, each measure has certain limitations beyond those of the associated level of measurement. The mean can be skewed by extreme scores at either end of the distribution. This can be seen in the sample data used due to the city of Boston's higher victimization rate. With that extreme score of 86 auto thefts per 1000 citizens removed, the mean is reduced from 34.6 to 30.3. In instances where such extreme scores (called outliers) are prevalent, the median may be the preferred measure of central tendency. The median also has limitations. It does not reflect any values in a data set other than the middle scores. Moreover, it sometimes only provides an approximate median value if there are ties in the middle range. This problem is present in the example used above. Although 32 was the median, with six positions below it, only five values were above it due to the second value of 32 in the distribution. Finally, the mode can be plagued by multiple modal values, thus not describing the middle of the distribution very well. The example, in fact, was bimodal. Also, two or more extreme scores can represent a mode that is very misleading. Due to these limitations, measures of central tendency need to be examined very carefully and in conjunction with measures of dispersion.

Measures of Dispersion

Measures of dispersion further describe a set of data, complementing what is communicated by measures of central tendency. While the latter provide some picture of the "middle" of a distribution, the former reflect how the scores spread around the mean. That spread of scores is referred to as dispersion or variability. Measures of dispersion can be very important descriptors because identical measures of central tendency can be associated with dramatically different dispersions as shown in Figure 4.8. Distribution a reflects wide dispersion around the mean, while b illustrates a case of little dispersion around it.

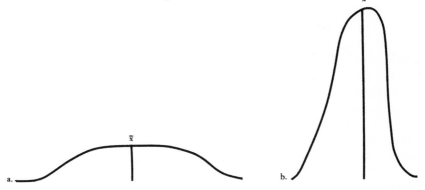

Figure 4.8 Small Versus Large Dispersion Around the Mean

The range is the simplest measure of dispersion or variability and can be reported for ordinal or higher level data. It is the number that expresses the difference between the highest and lowest values in a distribution. It is calculated by subtracting the lowest score in a distribution from the highest and adding one. In the example of victimization data, the highest number was 86 and the lowest was 15. The formula for the range in this case is 86-15+1=72. The range of the distribution is 72. One problem with this measure is that it is subject to dramatic effects by outliers. So again, if the city of Boston is removed from the sample data set, the range is reduced to 43-15+1=29. A range of 29 communicates something very different than does a range of 72. To prevent such distortions, the interquartile range (Q) is often calculated. Q is the range spanning the first to third quartiles ($Q_3 - Q_1$). It is calculated by multiplying n by .75 and .25 respectively to locate the positions of Q_3 and Q_1, subtracting their associated values and adding one. Q would be calculated for the victimization data as follows:

1. Q_3 = .75 x 13 = 9.75
   = 10th position
   = 38

2. Q_1 = .25 x 13 = 3.25
   = 3rd position
   = 25

$$3. Q = Q - Q_1 + 1$$
$$= 38 - 25 + 1$$
$$= 14$$

Both R and Q fail to utilize information from all scores in a distribution. The variance and standard deviation, however, are based on interval/ratio level data and incorporate every value in a distribution. The variance (S^2 for a sample; σ for a population) can be defined as the mean squared deviation from the mean, while the standard deviation (S for a sample; σ for a population) is simply the square root of the variance. When actually calculating the variance and standard deviation, computational formulas will be used or more typically the researcher will acquire these statistics from the printouts of a canned computer program. However, to understand the underlying concepts, the definitional formula should be examined carefully. Below is the definitional formula for S^2 :

$$S^2 = \frac{\Sigma(X-\overline{X})^2}{n}$$

To calculate S, simply take the square root of S^2. The following example illustrates calculations of S^2 and S via the definitional formula:

Victimization Values	$X-\overline{X}$	$(X-\overline{X})^2$	
15	-19.6	384.2	
18	-16.6	275.6	
25	- 9.6	92.2	$\overline{X} = \frac{450}{13} = 34.6$
25	- 9.6	92.2	
29	- 5.6	31.4	
30	- 4.6	21.2	$S^2 = \frac{3812.8}{13}$
32	- 2.6	6.8	
32	- 2.6	6.8	$= 293.3$
36	1.4	2.0	$S = 17.1$
38	3.4	11.6	
41	6.4	41.0	
43	8.4	70.6	
86	51.4	2796.2	
450		3812.8	

Whenever the mean and the standard deviation of a distribution is known, the normal curve for that distribution can be constructed so that the various proportions of the distribution can be estimated from the area under the normal curve. For the example of victimization scores, the distribution would be projected as in Figure 4.9.

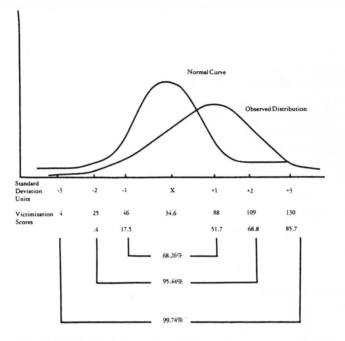

Figure 4.9 Skewed Distribution for Victimization Auto Theft Rates in 13 Cities

With S and S^2, the effects of the outlier are again seen. S is very large and when plotted on a curve, the result is a skewed distribution. Because n is very small, the extreme value of 86 has a disproportionate impact on S. As a sample, it suggests that σ would be likewise skewed. If the extreme score is eliminated and S recalculated (again rounding to one digit right of the decimal), it equals 8.25. Try recalculating it for practice. This new standard deviation is plugged into the normal curve in Figure 4.10.

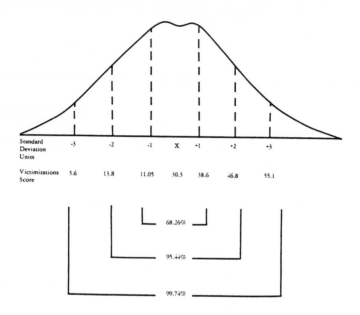

Standard Deviation Units	-3	-2	-1	X	+1	+2	+3
Victimizations Score	5.6	13.8	11.05	30.3	38.6	46.8	55.1

68.26%

95.44%

99.74%

Figure 4.10 Distribution Closely Approximating Normal for Victimization Auto theft Rates in 12 Cities

Other than being bimodal (modes just above and below $\overline{X}$), this distribution now approximates the normal curve rather closely. In this situation S may be useful to establish confidence levels and intervals. For example, viewing the 12 victimization rates as a sample, we could be 95 percent confident that the true average victimization auto theft rate for the population of cities is between 13.8 and 46.8 per thousand citizens. To reduce that confidence interval further toward a useful level would require a substantial increase of n.

Measures of Frequency

Frequency distributions are used to summarize and display counts of data. A frequency distribution identifies the number (frequency) of cases for each attribute (category) of a variable and usually the percent of the whole represented by each. Table 4.1 provides an example for a nominal level variable.

Table 4.1 Number of Respondents by Sex

Sex	Frequency	Percent
Male	32	40.0
Female	48	60.0
Total	80	100.0

With ordinal or higher level data, a cumulative percent column is usually added as in Table 4.2. This facilitates cumulative summary statements. For example, one can see at a glance that 65 percent of the sample is under the age of 45.

Table 4.2 Number of Respondents by Age

Age	Frequency	Percent	Cumulative Percent
18-25	18	22.5	22.5
26-34	20	25.0	47.5
35-44	14	17.5	65.0
45-59	11	13.8	78.8
60+	17	21.2	100.0
Total	80	100.0	

Inferential Statistics

Discussions of the normal curve, probability theory and the law of large numbers from earlier in this chapter provide the framework for the last topic of data analysis. Researchers usually begin their analyses by calculating descriptive statistics for each variable. This is important because it focuses attention on problems such as outliers and skewed distributions, as well as providing both the researcher and consumer of the research with a feel for the data. However, most research in criminal justice ultimately focuses on the examination of a sample to draw inferences (generalizations) to a population. This important branch of statistics is called inferential statistics. Sometimes the researcher draws inferences from a sample to some finite and relatively small population, such as from a sample of 50 police officers to the total population of 350 officers in a given police department. At other times the population will be extremely large or even infinite as when a study of 50 police officers provides the basis for generalizing about police behavior in America. Another example would be conducting research on the deterrent effects of punishment and drawing generalizations from a group of college students to any potential law violators. Most criminal justice research also involves hypothesis testing - drawing inferences from a sample statistic reflecting relationships between variables to a population parameter. The remainder of this chapter reviews this process for some common inferential statistics appropriate for nominal, ordinal and interval/ratio level data.

Parametric and Nonparametric Statistics

Parametric statistics are based on interval/ratio level measurements of the data. Their use is limited by various assumptions concerning the distributions from which they are drawn. The assumptions of parametric statistics are:

1. Independent observations.
2. Statistics are drawn from normally distributed
      populations.
3. The populations must have equal variances.
4. The effects must be additive.
5. The measures must be derived from an interval
      or ratio scale.

Nonparametric statistics are distribution free. They are used to analyze nominal and ordinal level data. They are less powerful statistics, but much data in the criminal justice field is inherently nominal or ordinal, thus necessitating their use. Siegel's (1956) *Nonparametric Statistics* should be consulted as the classic reference for any of these statistics.

Statistical Proofs

A complete statistical proof always must answer each of the following questions:
1. Do differences exist that are statistically
      significant?
2. What is the strength (magnitude) of the
      differences?
3. What is the direction of the differences?
4. What is the nature of the differences?

Consequently, the student of research should remember that a complete proof always takes into consideration existence, strength, direction and nature. Existence is demonstrated by using the appropriate test of statistical significance. Strength will be determined by using a measure of association. Direction is determined from the sign (either positive or negative) of a statistical test or examination of the data as cast into a contingency table. Nature is determined from a scattergram and is appropriate only for interval/ratio level data. For existence, strength and direction, both parametric and nonparametric tests are available for each step in the statistical proof. Figure 4.11 presents a statistical analysis paradigm extending Siegel (1956) to summarize techniques available for a statistical proof. Five statistics from the paradigm for establishing existence, strength and direction and appropriate for nominal, ordinal and interval/ratio measures are then presented. For more detailed treatment of these statistics refer to Hy, Feig and Regoli (1983) or other social science statistics textbooks.

LEVEL	TYPE	ASSUMPTIONS	EXISTENCE	STRENGTH	DIRECTION	NATURE
NOMINAL	N O N P A R A M E T R I C	few	x^2	Frequencies Mode	Range	N/A
ORDINAL			F-Kruskal-Wallis F-Freedman Kolmogorov-Smirnov Mann-Whitney U	Rho-correlations Lambda Gamma E^2, W^2 Somer's D	Rho - +	
INTERVAL	P A R A M E T R I C	equal means equal variances independence randomly sampled interval measures	t (2 groups) F-ANOVA F - ANOCVA F - Regressions F - r^2 Z	Mean, Median Variance Standard Deviation r (correlations) r^2 as a PRE measure	r	Scattergram
RATIO						

Figure 4.11 Statistical Analysis Paradigm

Chi Square

The chi square (χ^2) test assumes only nominal level data. If data measured at higher levels are analyzed via χ^2, information is being "thrown away" and power lost. However, with nominal level data, χ^2 and its derivatives (*e.g.,* Cramers V and Phi square) are appropriate for testing hypotheses. What χ^2 determines is whether the pattern observed in sample data depart significantly from what would be expected in the population if X and Y were unrelated. The null hypothesis then, represents the frequencies expected when X and Y are unrelated (independent). The research (alternative) hypothesis represents differences between the "expected" and "observed" (actual) values or in other words, a situation where the variables are related (dependent).

The first step in conducting the χ^2 test is to cast the data into a contingency (also called crosstabulation) table. This table is a joint frequency distribution for the various attributes of the two variables. That is, it consists of a "cell" indicating the frequency of cases for each possible combination of X and Y attributes. It also displays "marginals" for each row and column of the table. These are the summed frequencies of each row and each column. The sum of the row frequencies and the sum of the column frequencies equal n. Since every variable must have a minimum of two attributes, the minimum contingency table is a 2x2. Lets look at an example. Consider the following hypothesis:

Ho: The victimization auto theft rate is *not* related to
population density.

Ha: The victimization auto theft rate *is* related to
population density.

The first step in testing the hypothesis is to cast the data into a contingency table. The data are at the interval level. Therefore, it is necessary to reduce them to categorical data. This was done for Table 4.3 below by dichotomizing at the mean of each variable.

TABLE 4.3 Relationships Between Victimization Auto Theft Rate
and Population Density for the 26 NCS Cities

Density

Auto Theft Rate		Low	High	Total
	Low	9	7	16
	High	4	6	10
	Total	13	13	26

Table 4.3 indicates that nine cities have both low population density and low victimization auto theft rates, while six are high on both variables. Conversely, it shows that four cities have high auto theft rates, yet are low on density and that seven have low auto theft rates while characterized by high density. These are the observed values. To test the hypothesis, they need to be compared to expected values, *i.e.,* what the joint frequencies would be if auto theft and population density were unrelated. Expected values are calculated by application of a simple rule:

MULTIPLY THE COMMON MARGINALS
AND DIVIDE BY n

So for cell one (upper left hand corner), 13 x 16/26 = 8. Cell two has the same row and column marginals and thus the same expected values. Cell three (lower left hand corner) yields an expected value of 13 x 10/26 = 5 and cell four is the same. The observed and expected values are all that are needed for the χ^2 formula:
$$\Sigma(O-E)^2/E$$

Chi square is easily calculated as follows:

O	E	O-E	$(O-E)^2$	$(O-E)^2/E$
9	8	1	1	.125
7	8	-1	1	.125
4	5	-1	1	.20

| 6 | 5 | 1 | 1 | .20 |

$$\overline{\Sigma\,.65}$$

The chi square value must be located on a distribution table to determine whether or not it is significant. See Hy, Feig and Regoli (1983) or most other social science statistics texts for the X^2 distribution table. For a 2x2 table, X^2 must equal or exceed a value of 3.84 to be significant at the .05 level. Since our X^2 value is only .65, the null hypothesis is retained. The observed and expected values are not different enough to support a conclusion that population density and victimization auto theft rates are related.

In sum, chi square tests for the existence of a relationship. It is nondirectional, but direction can be determined by examination of the contingency table. The chi square test can also be followed by tests of the strength of relationships such as Cramer's V and Phi square (Hy, Feig and Regoli, 1983). An important limitation that should be kept in mind when using X^2 is that all expected values must equal or exceed five, as lower values can generate spurious results.

Gamma

The Gamma (γ) statistic assumes ordinal level measurement and therefore utilizes ranking information. It is equal to the proportion of all possible pairs of cases that reflect a positive or negative relationship. Thus, it indicates the direction of a relationship, ranging from 1.0 to -1.0. As a measure of strength, it is a proportionate reduction in error (PRE) statistic. This means that with knowledge of X, error in guessing the values of Y is reduced by the γ proportion. For example, if $\gamma = .30$, then error in predicting Y values is reduced by 30 percent relative to predictions with no knowledge of X.

Gamma is easy to calculate, particularly with small contingency tables. The formula is:

$$(S-O)/(S+O)$$

S represents the number of pairs with the same (concordant or positive) ranking, while O represents the number of pairs with the opposite (discordant or negative) ranking. S is calculated by multiplying n for each cell by the sum of n for all cells below and to the right of it. Using Table 4.3 as an example, S = 9x6=54 and O = 4x7=28. Substituting these values in the γ formula we have:

$$\Upsilon = (54-28)/(54+28)$$
$$= 26/82$$
$$= .32$$

This reflects a positive relationship with a 32 percent error reduction in predicting auto theft rates from population density. That is, it tells us that if we always guess that a city with high population density has high victimization rates reported for auto theft and that those with low density are low on auto theft, we will predict 32 percent better overall than our best guess with no knowledge of population density.

Gamma has some disadvantages. It does not demonstrate existence of a relationship per se as it applies no statistical test of significance. Moreover, as a measure of association it tends to be inflated. For this reason, some statisticians recommend application of Tau_c (Hy, Feig and Regoli, 1983).

Correlation Coefficient

The Pearson correlation coefficient (r) requires interval or ratio data. It is a powerful measure of the extent to which a group of cases occupy the same relative position on two variables. After r is calculated, its value and n can be applied to a significance table to draw conclusions regarding the existence of a relationship in the population. The strength of the relationship is then determined by a PRE interpretation of r^2. Direction is reflected in the range of r from 1.0 to -1.0. Finally, most computer statistical packages will plot scattergrams in conjunction with the calculation of r. This facilitates visual inspection of the relationship which may reveal important details. For example, r assumes a linear (straight line) relationship and is attenuated to the extent that the data are characterized by curvilinearity. Figure 4.12 contrasts examples of linear and curvilinear relationships.

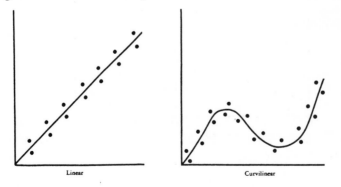

Linear   Curvilinear

Figure 4.12 Examples of Linear and Curvilinear Scattergrams

The following is the definitional formula for r, often referred to as the mean deviation method of calculation:

$$r = \frac{\Sigma xy}{\sqrt{\Sigma x^2 \cdot \Sigma y^2}}$$

where $x = (X - \bar{X})$
$y = (Y - \bar{Y})$

Consider the hypothesis that the rates of automobile theft as reported to the police and as reported in victimization surveys are correlated. This hypothesis could be tested by correlating the two measures. The existence of a relationship would be determined by the significance level, while strength would be reflected in r . Of course, the direction of the relationship should be positive if the two indicators are measuring the same phenomenon and the greater the magnitude of r, the more confidence one would have that they are measuring the same thing. This example is worked below via the mean deviation method. The raw data are found on page 47. The auto theft rates for the UCR data were calculated by the formula:

$$\frac{\text{Number of Thefts}}{\text{Population}} \text{ X } 1000$$

City	X	x	X²	Y	y	y²	xy
1	28.1	16.2	262.4	86.0	48.6	2362.0	787.3
2	9.7	-2.2	4.8	30.0	-7.4	54.8	16.3
3	5.8	-6.1	37.2	25.0	-12.4	153.8	75.6
4	9.8	-2.1	4.4	32.0	-5.4	29.2	11.3
5	8.2	-3.7	13.7	18.0	-19.4	376.4	71.8
6	7.3	-4.6	21.2	29.0	-8.4	70.6	38.6
7	10.6	-1.3	1.7	41.0	3.6	13.0	-4.7
8	10.7	-1.2	1.4	32.0	-5.4	29.2	6.5
9	13.1	1.2	1.4	36.0	-1.4	2.0	-.2
10	12.7	.8	.6	43.0	5.6	31.4	4.5
11	6.5	-5.4	29.2	25.0	-12.4	29.8	67.0
12	13.0	1.1	1.2	38.0	.6	.4	.7
13	6.2	-5.7	32.5	15.0	-22.4	501.8	127.7
14	8.1	-3.8	14.4	28.5	-8.9	79.2	33.8
15	9.9	-2.0	4.0	35.0	-2.4	5.8	4.8
16	26.4	14.5	210.3	76.3	38.9	1513.2	564.0
17	8.2	-3.7	13.7	24.4	-13.0	169.0	48.1
18	13.8	1.9	3.6	44.4	7.0	49.0	13.3
19	18.1	6.9	47.6	36.9	-.5	.3	-3.5
20	9.8	-2.1	4.4	33.9	-3.5	12.3	7.4
21	19.1	7.2	51.8	47.3	9.9	98.0	71.3
22	9.6	-2.3	5.3	36.0	-1.4	2.0	3.2
23	13.6	1.7	2.9	49.0	11.6	134.6	19.7
24	12.0	.1	.0	42.0	4.6	21.2	.5
25	9.6	-2.3	5.3	26.0	-11.4	130.0	26.2
26	8.2	-3.7	13.7	42.0	4.6	21.2	-17.0
	$\bar{x}$=11.9		788.7	$\bar{y}$=37.4		5890.2	1974.2

where X = UCR auto theft rate per thousand population
Y = NCS auto theft rate per thousand population

$$r = \sqrt{\frac{1974.2}{(788.7) \quad (5890.2)}}$$

$$= .92$$

The significance of r can be found in a table of critical values in an appendix to most statistics texts. With r = .92 and n at 26, the correlation is significant beyond the .001 level. Consequently, the null hypothesis is rejected and it is concluded that a relationship does exist. It is also positive in direction as predicted. The strength of the relationship, expressed in terms of r^2 indicates that approximately 85 percent of the variation in one measure is explained by the other. Thus, one would probably conclude that these two measures of automobile theft are interchangeable. If a scattergram is plotted, the researcher has addressed all four phases of a statistical proof.

t Test

The t test measures the difference between two means, thus requiring interval or ratio level data. One variation of the t test applies to the one-sample situation. In this case the researcher desires to compare a sample $\overline{X}$ with a pre-established value. For example, a corrections commissioner might wish to contrast the $\overline{X}$ square feet per inmate in his/her institutions with a standard recommended by the American Correctional Association. A more common research situation is the two-sample or t test for independent samples. Here the researcher is comparing the means of two samples derived from two independent groups. The formula for t is:

$$t = \frac{\overline{X}_1 - \overline{X}_2}{SE}$$

However, several steps are required in the computations. As an example of the t test for independent samples, suppose the director of a police academy wants to introduce a new fitness program and determine if it leads to significantly lower heart rates among those who complete it compared to those who complete the traditional program. Twenty recruits are divided into two groups and following the fitness programs register the following heart rates:

$\underline{X}_1$	$\underline{X}_2$
64	69
58	72
61	65
68	67
49	58
65	66

59	62
68	70
62	70
57	68

The hypothesis would be:

$$H_o: \quad X_1 \geq X_2$$
$$H_a: \quad X_1 < X_2$$

where X_1 = average heart rate of participants in new fitness
                program
        X_2 = average heart rate of participants in old fitness
                program

To test the hypothesis, calculate the value of t by the following steps:
  1. For *each* sample compute n, $\overline{X}$ and S.
     For X_1 these values are 10, 61 and 5.4.
     For X_2 they are 10, 67 and 4.
  2. Compute the *pooled* estimate of the standard deviation.
     The computational formula is:
     $$S = \sqrt{[n_1 (S_1^2) + n_2 (S_2^2)] / (n_1 + n_2)}$$
     The formula yields an estimate of 4.78 for the
     example.
  3. Compute the standard error. The computational
     formula is:
     $$SE = \sqrt{1 / (n_1 - 1) + 1 / (n_2 - 1)}$$
     The standard error for the example is 2.25.

Now, substituting these values in the t formula, we have:
$$t = \frac{61 - 67}{2.25}$$

$$= 2.66$$

After t is calculated, a table designed for the t statistic (found in an appendix to most statistics texts) must be used to determine whether or not it is statistically significant. Whenever statistical significance is established, the conclusion that the researcher can draw is that differences exist between the means of the two groups. The direction is evident when the group the means of the two groups. The direction is evident when the group means are examined. However, further statistical tests are necessary to describe the strength and/or nature of the differences. In the example, reference to the t distribution table reveals that a t of 2.66 (one-tailed test) is significant at the .01 level. Thus, the null hypothesis is rejected at that level and the conclusion is that the heart rates of those completing the new fitness program are significantly lower than that of those who completed the traditional program.

F Test

The F test is an extention of t, comparing the means of three or more groups. The computations for F are quite complex and will not be reviewed. It is actually associated with three advanced statistical techniques that are often used in criminal justice research: Analysis of Variance (ANOVA), Analysis of Covariance (ANCOVA) and multiple regression. Each yields an F value which can be referred to an F table to determine statistical significance. For ANOVA and ANCOVA, the dependent variables must be measured at the interval or ratio levels. However, when F is calculated in conjunction with multiple regression, it is quite common to see categorical and interval level independent variables in an equation. The categorical variables are referred to as dummy variables in this case and research has revealed that regression techniques remain very powerful even with categorical variables. A major reference for ANOVA and ANCOVA is Hays (1973). Those who are planning multiple regression analysis should consult Kerlinger and Pedhazur (1973).

Exercises

1. Select a topic on which you are interested in conducting research. State a null and research hypothesis for the proposed research. What would Type I and II errors be in this example?

2. Identify rival hypotheses for your topic.

3. How can each of the variables in your hypothesis be measured? What is the level of measurement?

4. Using the number of rapes recorded in the UCRs (data on page 46), calculate the *rate* of this crime for each of the 26 cities.

5. For the UCR rate of rape that you calculated, what is the $\bar{X}$, Md and Mo? What is the R and Q? Calculate S and S_2. Collapse the data as appropriate and record them in a cumulative frequency distribution.

6. Calculate the UCR auto theft *rate* for each of the 26 cities.

7. What relationship would you hypothesize to exist between the UCR rape and auto theft rates? Why? State your hypothesis in terms of a null and research hypothesis.

8. Calculate r and explain what conclusion it supports regarding your hypothesis.

9. Collapse these two crime rates as appropriate and cast the data in a 2x2 contingency table. Calculate χ^2 and γ. What conclusions do they support? If any different conclusions are supported by these three statistics, why?

10. Describe situations in which the t and F statistics would be appropriate.

References

Asher, Herbert B. *Causal Modeling* (Beverly Hills: Sage Publications, 1976).

Campbell, Donald and Julian Stanley *Experimental and Quasi-Experimental Designs for Research* (Chicago: Rand McNally College Publishing Company, 1966).

Cohen, J. *Statistical Power Analysis for the Behavioral Sciences* (New York: Academic Press, 1977).

Cook, Thomas and Donald Campbell *Quasi-Experimentation: Design and Analysis for Field Settings* (Chicago: Rand McNally College Publishing Company, 1979).

Hays, William L. *Statistics for the Social Sciences* (New York: Holt, Rinehart and Winston, Inc., 1973).

Hy, Ronald; Feig, Douglas and Robert Regoli *Research Methods and Statistics* (Cincinnati: Anderson Publishing Company, 1983).

Kerlinger, Fred and Elazar Pedhazur *Multiple Regression in Behavioral Research* (New York: Holt, Rinehart and Winston, Inc., 1973).

Kish, Leslie *Survey Sampling* (New York: John Wiley and Sons, 1965).

Rosenberg, Morris *The Logic of Survey Analysis* (New York: Basic Books, Inc., Publishers, 1968).

Siegel, Sidney *Nonparametric Statistics for the Behavioral Sciences* (New York: McGraw-Hill Book Company, 1956).

5
The Computer as a Tool

The computer is one of the most important tools of the criminal justice researcher. Every student and practitioner of criminal justice should be aware of their capabilities and be "computer literate." Actually, the computer is used for many purposes in criminal justice other than research. For example, agency payrolls, personnel records and budgets are computerized. In police departments crime analyses are conducted, dispatching computer assisted and crime records maintained. Court records are computerized and probation and parole officers maintain caseload records on computers. In sum, the computer is a vital component of contemporary criminal justice practice. However, the focus of this chapter is on the computer as a tool of the criminal justice researcher. It will demonstrate how to use the computer for the analysis of your data.

The first step to making use of the computer as a tool is to learn basic *computerese* - the language of computers. Words such as *hardware*, *software*, *canned* and many others are essential concepts to communicate regarding computer use. As a researcher who needs to put the computer to work for you, there are two other primary areas that must be known initially. First, what type of machinery is available to access the computer? This can be as different as the use of cardpunch medium to communicate with a large free standing computer, or a remote network computer, or it may refer to the use of interactive terminals to communicate with the computer. It may also include the availability of microcomputers in the department or at home. Each student will need to find out what is available and what is being used at his or her particular school. One of the best ways to do this is to elect to take an introductory course in computer science.

Second, what computer language is being used at your school? There are many languages, each with its own particular strengths. There are primary languages (*e.g.* FORTRAN, COBOL, BASIC) and canned languages (*e.g.* SPSS-X, SAS, BMD). A canned language is actually a package of prewritten programs utilizing natural English-like commands that can be mastered with relative ease. The typical student undertaking criminal justice research will use a canned language, although it will be helpful to learn FORTRAN which serves as the primary language for many canned packages. The most widely used canned language for social science research is SPSS-X. *(SPSS-X is a trademark of SPSS Incorporated of Chicago, Illinois, for its proprietary computer software.)* The package is available on the mainframe computer(s) of most colleges and universities and recently has been made avaiable for minicomputers as well. This chapter will review the basics of setting up an SPSS-X job and interpeting the output.

Setting Up An SPSS-X Job

An SPSS-X program or job consists of a detailed set of instructions written in natural language which is self-contained. That is, it has complete instructions from start to finish of a run. It petitions the computer to call an already-written problem-solving program and to apply certain statistical manipulative functions for the purpose of description and/or inference. A set of data is included in or retrieved by the program. A complete program or job is most readily conceptualized as a deck of 80 column IBM cards submitted to a card reader. Each card is simply a line on an interactive terminal. Viewed in this manner, an SPSS-X job consists of three subparts or sets of cards called files as follows:
1. An access file
2. A control file
3. A data file

The access file (sometimes called the Job Control Language or JCL cards) usually specifies the following:
1. Control codes that allow the user entry to
   the computer system and charges the time
   used to the appropriate account.
2. Which computer will be used.
3. What language will be used.
Access files are always specific to the local computer installation. In order to obtain the information as to how this file should be written, consult your professor or the staff of your computer or research center.

The control file in SPSS-X performs the following functions:
1. Names the file being created.
2. Specifies variables and parameters.
3. Instructs the computer to execute the
   requested statisticalfunctions.

Finally, the data file consists of the raw data to be analyzed. It may be included in the deck (or keyed in at a terminal) or instructions specifying its location (*i.e.,* on disk or tape) may be included in the control file. It is the control file that instructs the computer how to read the data and what to do with them.

The first step to learning SPSS-X is to gain access to the *SPSS-X User's Guide* (SPSS Incorporated, 1983). This manual provides extensive documentation, yet is written in such a manner that the computer neophyte can learn to prepare jobs. Start by reading the first three chapters of the manual, paying particular attention to the sample jobs and job segments. Then select those chapters delineating the procedures for specific statistical analyses appropriate for your study. Most colleges and universities have short courses or seminars available to introduce the student to SPSS-X. Most computer centers also have summary handouts available to assist the beginner in job setup. Both of these resources should be taken advantage of, if available. Finally, practice is important. New users will make a lot of mistakes leading to error messages. Doing the necessary detective work to solve this is one of the best ways to learn.

The primary advantages of using a computer for statistical analyses are phenomenal increases in speed and accuracy. Canned programs such as SPSS-X make complex statistical analyses with massive data sets within the reach of even beginning researchers. This provides fantastic opportunity, but also requires some cautions. A computer will perform only those functions that it is programmed for, but if programmed for inappropriate tasks they will still be performed. In fact, the computer is so easy to use that researchers sometimes use it to perform analyses that they do not fully comprehend or will use data of questionable validity. But only the researcher is responsible for the quality of the data and the interpretation of the statistics - not the computer! The researcher must think the entire research process through and recognize the computer for what it is - a tool to assist them in the manipulation and analysis of data.

Let's now set up a simple SPSS-X job that will conduct some of the statistical analyses reviewed in Chapter 4. The sample set of data will include measures of the index crime and clearance rates, the population and total number of index crimes committed in the 35 independent cities of Virginia. These data were derived from the Virginia Uniform Crime Reporting Program (1975) and the *County and City Data Book* (1972) of the Census Bureau.

The first few cards of your deck (or lines on a terminal) will comprise the access file specific to your computer installation. Following them, punch the following cards to run the sample SPSS-X program.

1   TITLE EXAMPLE 5.1

This first SPSS-X card will generate the assigned title (EXAMPLE 5.1 in this case) to be printed at the top of each page of your output. A maximum of 60 characters may be used in the title.

2   DATA LIST/CRIME 1-5   CLEAR 6-9
      POPU 18-23   TOTCRI 47-51

The second card provides the names for each variable and their column location. Variable names may consist of a maximum of eight characters and must start with a letter. Use abbreviated variable names that communicate what the data are. In this case, columns 1-5 contain the index crime rate and columns 6-9 the index clearance rate. Population for the cities is recorded in columns 18-23, while the raw (total) number of index crimes is recorded in columns 47-51. The SPSS-X printout will summarize how the data are being read in the program. For the sample run, the following should appear immediately after the data list card.

The above Data List Statement will read   1 Records from File inline.

Variable	Rec	Start	End		Format	Width	Dec.
Crime	1	1	5		F	5	0
Clear	1	6	9		F	4	0
Popu	1	18	23		F	6	0
TotCri	1	47	51		F	5	0

End of Datalist Table.

3   VARIABLE LABELS CRIME 'CRIMES PER THOUSAND
      POPULATION'
4   CLEAR 'POLICE CLEARANCE RATE'
5   POPU 'POPULATION OF CITY'
6   TOTCRI 'TOTAL NUMBER OF CRIMES'

Cards 3-6 assign extended variable labels. These labels may be up to 40 characters in length and will generate these labels on some output.

7   LIST

This is a procedure command that instructs the computer to list all data contained in the data file. Only one procedure command may precede the data.

- BEGIN DATA

This card informs the computer that it will now encounter the data, which have been defined by the preceding cards. In the sample deck, it is followed by 35 data cards. Note that the data do not occupy fields that are side-by- side in this sample. You may wish to

- BEGIN DATA

This card informs the computer that it will now encounter the data, which have been defined by the preceding cards. In the sample deck, it is followed by 35 data cards. Note that the data do not occupy fields that are side-by- side in this sample. You may wish to move POPU to columns 10-15 and TOTCRI to 16-20, but if you do so be sure that this is reflected in the DATA LIST card. Below is the output of this program, reproducing (listing) the entire data file.

Example 5.1

CRIME	CLEAR	POPU	TOTCRI
7.87	77.9	7957	59
47.89	20.0	172106	10397
45.67	26.1	24504	1023
20.27	25.6	6889	152
63.10	28.0	36103	2846
39.78	25.1	4001	179
75.69	25.2	307951	22721
56.13	25.2	138177	7970
56.38	26.6	19653	1105
56.87	28.8	54083	3162
34.12	42.2	6278	232
24.64	38.4	10060	239
25.87	28.4	15097	489
32.36	26.9	5501	178
80.95	35.1	38880	3408
17.75	47.6	6425	126
92.11	15.4	14643	1879
60.10	15.8	9069	625
52.79	14.0	16707	908
41.26	21.8	9858	2001
49.65	15.9	21982	1147
96.73	23.9	92115	8715
83.66	23.3	249621	20246
25.24	9.2	11596	313
68.31	21.2	110963	7767
42.56	20.3	23471	1064
42.46	19.9	14605	726
49.34	19.0	120779	6538
71.49	15.5	14450	1201
85.39	21.4	10772	982
80.26	9.9	21970	1846
37.89	21.7	46391	1845
46.52	12.7	89580	4783
37.15	23.1	14857	717
81.48	16.6	110938	9778

Number of Cases Read = 35

Number of Cases Listed = 35

- END DATA

This card follows the last data card, signalling the computer that all data have been read. Neither the BEGIN DATA or END DATA card will be assigned a number on the printout of the program. However, the next card will be numbered nine.

9 CONDESCRIPTIVE ALL

This is the second procedure in this run. It instructs the computer to calculate and print descriptive statistics for all variables in the data file. Additional statistics and options can be requested by following this and most other statistical procedure commands with STATISTICS and OPTIONS cards.

10 PEARSON CORR CRIME WITH CLEAR

This is the third procedure of the run. It instructs the computer to calculate and print the value of r, n and the associated significance level. Additional statistics and options may be requested. The SPSS-X control file will be followed by additional JCL cards to signal the end of the run and relinquish access to the computer. This completes the description of a complete SPSS-X job including three distinct procedures: a list of the complete data file (output presented above so your data file may be punched), descriptive statistics for all variables and the correlation between the crime and clearance rates. The next section will discuss the interpretation of output from the latter two procedures and review additional analytical tasks from Chapter 4 that can easily be accomplished with SPSS-X.

Interpreting SPSS-X Output

Ultimately the art of quantitative research is the correct interpretation of the computer printout. It is not difficult to program statistical proofs or to read the printout's findings. Telling others what these findings mean is the art. At this point, the researcher is the only one responsible for his or her interpretations. Logical interpretations supported by quantitative findings will help construct a convincing argument from which a fact can be suggested, replicated, and ultimately proven.

After the computer program has been written and debugged (corrected) it should run. When a program has run, the computer produces a printout of the results. This printout may be very succinct or it may actually be hundreds of pages long. The student must know what is important to the statistical proof on the printout and what can be scanned quickly.

Many students have trouble understanding the computer printout. They become confused with the great mass of data that is reported. When canned progams are used, the printouts tend to be much longer and to include much information that the researcher did not request. Consequently each student needs to know what to look for and how to interpret the results that he or she has. This is where a basic knowledge of statistics is essential.

When a printout is examined the student should look for evidence of each of the steps in the statistical proof. He or she should not get lost in the vast amount of numbers that are reported. The key to printout interpretation is learning how to separate the information reported from the information needed.

Throughout this discussion SPSS-X canned programs have been examined. In the SPSS-X printout there are some important facts to remember. Among these are:

1. Significance levels are reported numerically.
2. The readability of the program is dependent on how well the program has been written; that is, how the variables have been labeled.
3. When errors are present, SPSS-X will find and print them. This error identification procedure is *seldom wrong*; therefore, it is important that students check printouts with reported errors very carefully.

Now let's turn to the output generated by the CONDESCRIPT-IVE command. Note that the name for each variable is listed on the extreme left and its label provided on the extreme right. For each variable, five descriptive statistics were listed. Remember that these statistics are provided by default with the CONDESCRIPTIVE command, but that more are available. First is the mean ($\bar{X}$) for each variable. Calculate some by hand as a check. The computer performed *all* of the calculations summarized in this table in 0.16 seconds! How long did it take you to calculate just $\bar{X}$ for one variable? Next is the standard deviation (S) for each variable. For practice and proof of the computer's speed and accuracy, calculate S for one variable. Next observe the lowest (minimum) and highest (maximum) value for each variable. For example, the lowest index crime is eight per 100,000 citizens, while the highest is 97. Thus, the range is 97-8+1=90. Finally, the valid N of cases for each variable is indicated.

Example 5.1

NUMBER OF VALID OBSERVATIONS (LISTWISE) = 35.00

Variable	Mean	Std Dev	Minimum	Maximum	Valid N	Label
CRIME	52.278	22.772	8	97	35	Crimes per Thousand Population
CLEAR	25.020	12.425	9	78	35	Police Clearance Rate
POPU	53086.629	71838.732	4001	307951	35	Population of City
TOTCRI	3639.057	5384.530	59	22721	35	Total Number of Crimes

Remember that the calculation of the correlation coefficient r requires interval level data. That assumption is met with the crime and clearance rates. The SPSS-X output (by default) displays three items: the value of r, the N of cases and the probability (significance) level. In the output below, observe that r is negative. Recall that this indicates that as clearance rates go up, crime rates go down or conversely, that as crime rates go up, clearance rates go down. Unfortunately, causal order is not addressed by correlations. The value of r is .2164, which indicates that 21.64 percent of variance in one variable is explained by the other. Finally, the significance level of .002 indicates that there are only two chances in one thousand that a correlation this strong among 35 cases could be observed by chance. Thus, in rejecting the null hypothesis that crime and clearance rates are unrelated, there are only two chances in one thousand of a Type I error. By default the significance test assumes a directional (one-tailed) research hypothesis.

Example 5.1

PEARSON CORRELATION COEFFICIENTS

CLEAR

CRIME   -.4652
(35)
P = .002

(Coefficient/(Cases)/1-Tailed Sig)   "." is printed if a coefficient cannot be computed.

Additional runs can be undertaken to carry out other tasks or additional procedures could have been included in the first run. First, let's continue the correlational analysis. Recall that the correlation is the only statistical technique reviewed in Chapter 4 that addresses all four components of a statistical proof. Three were addressed above, with only the nature of the relationship left unexamined. The nature of the relationship is revealed by a scattergram which can be generated for the sample data by the command:

SCATTERGRAM CRIME CLEAR

This card will replace the first procedure card (LIST) from the previous run. It may also be desirable to change the title specified on the TITLE card. Remove the other procedures following the data and run the scattergram. It looks like this:

Example 5.2

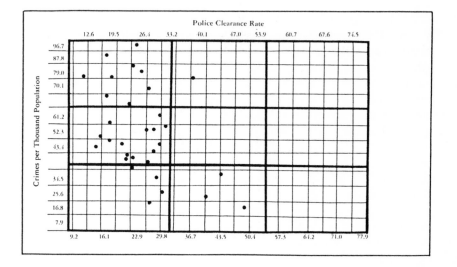

Note that each of the 35 cities is plotted at the intersection of the crime and clearance rate axes. There is no evidence of curvilinearity in the data. That is, if they were fit to a line, it would be a straight-line relationship that drops on the crime as it increases on the clearance axis. This represents a negative relationship as reflected in r. There is, however, one feature of the nature of this relationship that this scattergram alerts the researcher to. Note that there are a few outliers that inflate the value of r. One case in particular appears in the extreme lower right hand corner (representing values of 8 on crime and 78 on clearance rates). Should r be recalculated with this case removed, it would be closer to a zero value. A good researcher would observe this outlier and examine the specific case to determine if there were any reason to suspect its validity.

Let's examine one more SPSS-X job to demonstrate additional analytical techniques reviewed in Chapter 4. This output is labeled EXAMPLE 5.3 by so designating on the TITLE card. The first procedure requested will be a frequency distribution for all four variables. The command for this is:

7   FREQUENCIES VARIABLES = ALL/
8   FORMAT = NEWPAGE/
9   HISTOGRAM/

Card 7 (following the last variable label card of the sample program) requests a frequency distribution for all variables. Card 8 instructs the computer to go to a new page to print each table in the output. Finally, card 9 requests that each frequency distribution be accompanied by a histogram. Below is the output for police clearance rates among the 35 cities.

Example 5.3

CLEAR		POLICE CLEARANCE RATE			
VALUE LABEL	Value	Frequency	Percent	Valid Percent	Cum Percent
	9.2	1	2.9	2.9	2.9
	9.9	1	2.9	2.9	5.7
	12.7	1	2.9	2.9	8.6
	14.0	1	2.9	2.9	11.4
	15.4	1	2.9	2.9	14.3
	15.5	1	2.9	2.9	17.1
	15.8	1	2.9	2.9	20.0
	15.9	1	2.9	2.9	22.9
	16.6	1	2.9	2.9	25.7
	19.0	1	2.9	2.9	28.6
	19.9	1	2.9	2.9	31.4
	20.3	1	2.9	2.9	34.3
	21.2	1	2.9	2.9	37.1
	21.4	1	2.9	2.9	40.0
	21.7	1	2.9	2.9	42.9
	21.8	1	2.9	2.9	45.7
	23.1	1	2.9	2.9	48.6
	23.3	1	2.9	2.9	51.4
	23.9	1	2.9	2.9	54.3
	25.1	1	2.9	2.9	57.1
	25.2	2	5.7	5.7	62.9
	25.6	1	2.9	2.9	65.7
	26.1	1	2.9	2.9	68.6
	26.6	1	2.9	2.9	71.4
	26.9	1	2.9	2.9	74.3
	28.0	2	5.7	5.7	80.0
	28.4	1	2.9	2.9	82.9
	28.8	1	2.9	2.9	85.7
	35.1	1	2.9	2.9	88.6
	38.4	1	2.9	2.9	91.4
	42.2	1	2.9	2.9	94.3
	47.6	1	2.9	2.9	97.1
	77.9	1	2.0	2.9	100.0
	Total	35	100.0	100.0	

Example 5. 3

CLEAR   POLICE CLEARANCE RATE

Count	Midpoint	One Symbol Equals Approximately .20 Occurrences
2	10.33	**********
2	13.67	**********
5	17.00	************************
7	20.33	**********************************
6	23.67	*****************************
7	27.00	**********************************
!	30.33	*****
1	33.67	*****
1	37.00	*****
0	40.33	
1	43.67	*****
1	47.00	*****
0	50.33	
0	53.67	
0	57.00	
0	60.33	
0	63.67	
0	67.00	
0	70.33	
0	73.67	
1	77.00	*****

```
          I....+....I....+..I.....+...I....+....I....+....I
          0   |   2     4      6      8     10
              Histogram Frequency
```

Valid Cases 35   Missing Casses 0

Observe that the frequency distribution indicates the frequency of each value that occurs one or more times in the data set. However, only clearance rates of 25.2 and 28 are repeated, each of which occurs twice. There is also a column indicating the percent of all cases accounted for by that value (with a second column that counts only valid cases). Finally, the cumulative percent column allows one to glean summary information with ease. For example, one could quickly observe that 57.1 percent of Virginia cities have clearance rates of 25 percent or less. The accompanying histogram divides the cases into 21 equal intervals (3.35 in this example). It depicts the grouping of most clearance rates in the categories with midpoints of 17.0, 20.3, 23.7 and 27.0. It also draws attention to the lone locale with the exceptionally high 78 percent clearance rate.

To complete this sample run, insert after the END DATA card the necessary cards to compute chi square and gamma for testing the hypothesis that crime and clearance rates are related. A total of six cards will be needed as follows:

11   RECODE CRIME (LOW THRU 52.2 = 0)(52.3 THRU
     HIGH = 1)
12   RECODE CLEAR (LOW THRU 25.0 = 0)(25.1 THRU
     HIGH = 1)
13   VALUE LABELS CRIME O 'LOW' 1 'HIGH' /
14   CLEAR O 'LOW' 1 'HIGH'
15   CROSSTABS CRIME BY CLEAR
16   STATISTICS 1, 8

Recall that chi square requires nominal or ordinal level data, while gamma requires an ordinal level of measurement. Since the crime and clearance variables in the sample data file are interval, they must be reduced to ordinal categories before either of these statistics can be calculated. This is accomplished via the RECODE commands. They dichotomize the two variables at the mean. Value labels are then created to identify values below the means as low and those above as high. Line (card) 15 requests a crosstabulation table for the crime and clear variables. Finally, the STATISTICS card (16) requests the two statistics desired. The following table is the result:

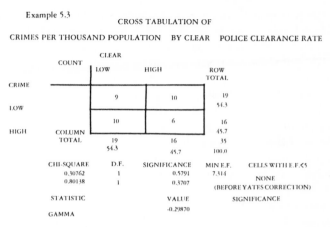

Example 5.3

CROSS TABULATION OF

CRIMES PER THOUSAND POPULATION   BY CLEAR   POLICE CLEARANCE RATE

Examine the table first. It reveals a *direction* consistent with the correlation coefficient. That is, there is some tendency for those cities low on crime to be high on clearance rates and vice versa. However, the pattern does not appear to be particularly strong. Consequently, chi square is small and nonsignificant. This difference is due to reducing the level of measurement. Remember that this process "throws away information" so that all distinction between cases is lost except whether they are characterized by low or high values on each variable. Consequently, power is lost and Type II errors become more likely. Of course the impact of any illegitimate outliers is also cancelled. Finally, look at the gamma value. It reflects a weak negative relationship which is more supportive of Ha than the chi square text, but less so than the correlation coefficient. This would be expected since the gamma formula incorporates rank order while chi square does not.

We have seen only a sample of SPSS-X capabilities. Almost any statistical analyses or data management procedures that the researcher may need are available in this software package. By studying the *User's Guide* and practicing, virtually any task can be completed.

Using The Microcomputer

The use of the microcomputer (personal computer) has grown dramatically in recent years. It is now possible for researchers with even very large data bases and the need for quite sophisticated statistical techniques to undertake all of their analyses on the minicomputer. A wide variety of statistical software is available to fit most needs and budgets. Some of the most sophisticated include SYSTAT, SPSS/PC and an example of a very modestly priced canned package for the Apple II+, IIe microcomputer is INTROSTAT 2.2, a Microcomputer Statistics Package for the Behavioral Sciences (a product of Ideal Systems, Fairfield, Iowa). This section will briefly review examples of tasks that can be accomplished with this package. The students should consult their campus computer laboratory to determine what microcomputer packages are available to them.

The INTROSTAT package, like most microcomputer software, is menu-driven and user friendly. To develop a data file, the user will first select DATA FILE MANAGEMENT on the main menu. The program will ask that you supply N and the number of variables to be included in the data file. Next, the DATA FILE MANAGEMENT menu will appear and DATA FILE CREATION should be selected. Numerous queries will follow: name of file, missing data code (*e.g.* -9), number of variables per case, variable labels and whether a case ID is desired. The data are then entered, case by case, for all variables. Afterward the user is given the opportunity to save the file on diskette for later use.

Once a file has been created with a microcomputer and saved to diskette, the contents should be verified. On INTROSTAT, this is easily accomplished via the LIST CASES on the INTROSTAT DATA FILE MANAGEMENT menu. This program requires that the data disk be in a drive, the data file name entered and several queries responded to regarding form of the desired output. The following output was generated for a file called demo containing the crime and popu data for the 35 Virginia cities.

DEMO CASES

| VAR# | | 1 | 2 |
LABEL ID		crime	popu
LOW		8	4001
HIGH		97	307951
CASE			
1	#1	7.87	7957
2	#2	47.89	172106
3	#3	45.67	24504
4	#4	20.27	6889
5	#5	63.1	36103
6	#6	39.78	4001
7	#7	75.69	307951
8	#8	56.13	138177
9	#9	56.38	19653
10	#10	56.87	54083
11	#11	34.12	6278
12	#12	24.64	10060
13	#13	25.87	15097
14	#14	32.36	5501
15	#15	80.95	38880
16	#16	17.75	6425
17	#17	92.11	14643
18	#18	60.1	9069
19	#19	52.79	16707
20	#20	41.26	9858
21	#21	49.65	21982
22	#22	96.73	92115
23	#23	83.66	249621
24	#24	25.24	11596
25	#25	68.31	110963
26	#26	42.56	23471
27	#27	42.46	14605
28	#28	49.34	120779
29	#29	71.49	14450
30	#30	85.39	10772
31	#31	80.26	21970
32	#32	37.89	46391
33	#33	46.52	89580
34	#34	37.15	14857
35	#35	81.48	110938

After checking content of the data file, a step that the researcher would be likely to next take is the generation of descriptive statistics on some or all of the variables. The following output was derived from the INTROSTAT package to describe the crime variable for the 35 cities.

DESCRIPTIVE STATS FOR ONE VARIABLE

CRIME

MIN = 7.87   MEAN = 52.28
MAX = 96.73   SD = 22.77
                     SE = 3.85

N = 35   0 MISSING

Numerous analytical procedures as well as data file management procedures are available on microcomputer software. INTROSTAT, for example, includes the following statistical procedures: crosstabulation, 9simple t-test, matched-pairs t-test, Man-Whitney U test, one and two-way ANOVA, correlations, scatterplots and simple linear regression. The following sample output shows r and n for the variable crime and popu. Note that the crime rates are positively correlated with the population of the cities. That is, there is a tendency for those cities with higher populations to have more reported index crimes per person than the cities of lower population. One would conclude that 17.6 percent (derived from r^2) of the crime variance is explained by population of the cities.

Example 5.1

PEARSON CORRELATIONS

	1.	2.
1. crime		.42
		35
2. popu		

For most research tasks the microcomputer will be found adequate. It may also be more convenient and economical. However, with extremely large data sets and/or with a need for much data manipulation, the mainframe may be more suitable. Of course what is available on any given campus will be a major determinant of the microcomputer versus mainframe decision as well. In either event, good luck with computing! It is really essential to adequate speed and accuracy in statistical analysis. It also becomes one of the most exciting and enjoyable aspects of the research process as one gains experience.

Exercises

1. Visit your computer center and find out what mainframe canned statistical packages are available. Find out what statistical packages are available for microcomputer use.

2. Use SPSS-X or another mainframe package to generate a full correlation matrix for the four variables in the sample data file. Do the same with a microcomputer package.

3. Use a mainframe package and a microcomputer package to compute crime rates for the cities from the POPU and TOTCRI variables.

4. Use a mainframe and a microcomputer package to collapse CRIME and POPU to categorical variables. Program the computer to cast them into a 2x2 contingency table and calculate chi square and gamma. Interpret the results.

5. Set up a control file for your own research project on both a mainframe and microcomputer package.

References

Bureau of the Census *County and City Data Book* (Washington D.C.: U.S. Government Printing Office, 1972).

SPSS, Inc. *SPSS-X User's Guide* (New York: McGraw-Hill Book Co.,1983).

Uniform Crime Reporting Program *Crime in Virginia* (Richmond, VA: Virginia State Police, 1975).

6

The Final Phase:
Publication and Presentation of Research

Research is reported to other scholars and students through the medium of oral presentation at a professional meeting and/or a manuscript published in a professional journal. In either case, it is important to understand the requirements for sound communication. Whether a research paper is to be presented to a professional society or submitted to a journal for publication consideration, a standard writing style should be followed in preparing the manuscript

There are a variety of styles that might be used to prepare a manuscript, each authorized by a different professional society or journal. These styles are typically described by a style sheet or manual available from the societies or printed on a special page set aside in the various journals. Most frequently used are those of the American Sociological Association and the American Psychological Association (APA). However, only the APA has a complete style manual which is available for reference. This manual is entitled *Publication Manual of the American Psychological Association* (APA, 1983). Students should develop the habit of using either it or another style manual. The styles required by leading professional journals such as *Criminology* (the official journal of the American Society of Criminology) and *Justice Quarterly* (the official journal of the Academy of Criminal Justice Sciences) are very similar to the APA style.

The format of this chapter will be to present each section of a research manuscript with illustrations from a student research paper.

Sections of a Research Manuscript

There are many steps in the preparation of a final manuscript draft. In the development of quality work, the following paradigm is offered.

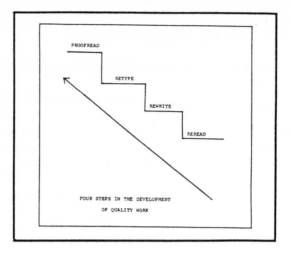

Other guidelines in preparing the manuscript include the following:
1. Research papers are considered professional
   papers. Each must have a professional
   appearance.
2. They must be typed on a good quality paper
   with uniform margins of 1 1/2 inches. Use
   standard size paper (8 1/2 x 11 inches).
3. All papers should be typed double spaced
   unless citing a long (in excess of six
   lines) quotation.
4. Indent five spaces for the first line of
   every paragraph. The only exception is
   the abstract which is typed without
   paragraph indentation.
5. Always write in third person, past tense.
6. Tables must be neatly typed and follow the
   prescribed format.
7. Whenever lines are drawn, a fine tip black
   ink pen must be used.

The sections of a research report typically include:
1. Title Page
2. Abstract
3. Introduction
4. Method
5. Results
6. Discussion

7. References
8. Appendices

Title Page
> The title page includes four parts: the title, author's name, author's affiliation, and running head.

A. Title
>   1. Summarize the main idea of the paper.
>   2. Identify the problem area, major variables
>   or theoretical issue and target
>   population.
>   3. The title should be clear and concise.
>   4. The title should be explanatory when
>   standing alone.
>   5. Type the title in all capital letters 18-24
>   lines from the top of the page. Center
>   the title. If there is more than one
>   line, double space between the lines.

B. Author's Name
>   1. Type your name(s) as formally used.
>   2. Omit titles and/or degrees.
>   3. Type your name(s) in capital and lower- case
>   letters four lines below the title.

C. Author's Affiliation
>   1. The author's affiliation is the institution
>   that the author represented at the time
>   of the research.
>   2. The institutional affiliation is typed in
>   capital and lowercase letters, centered,
>   one double-spaced line below the author's
>   name.

D. Running Head
>   1. The running head is an abbreviated title
>   used for editorial purposes.
>   2. It should not exceed 60 spaces including
>   punctuation and spaces between words.
>   3. The running head is typed, centered at about
>   eight lines from the bottom of the page.

It should be typed in capital and
lowercase letters.

```
         THE FATHER AND JUVENILE DELINQUENCY
                                              ⟵——— TITLE
         IN A NON-METROPOLITAN COMMUNITY


                Richard G. Bracewell ⟵——— AUTHOR'S
                                           NAME
               Valdosta State College⟵
                                        INSTITUTIONAL
                                        AFFILIATION
```

```
          Running Head:  Delinquency⟵——— RUNNING
                                          HEAD
```

Note: Richard G. Bracewell wrote this paper as an undergraduate
        student at Valdosta State College. Portions of it are
        used with permission of the author.

Abstract

1. The abstract is a brief summary of the content and purpose of the article. It is limited to between 150 and 200 words which allows the reader to quickly scan the primary points the researcher makes.

2. The abstract should be self-contained and fully intelligible without reference to the body of the paper.

3. Nothing should appear in the abstract that is not in the paper.

4. The abstract is the last part of the paper to be written since it is a paraphrase of the article.

5. The abstract should always answer these questions:
   - (A) What was studied?
   - (B) Who were the subjects?
   - (C) What was the method used?
   - (D) What were the primary findings?
   - (E) Why are these findings relevant?

6. The typing instructions for the abstract are:
   - (A) Begin on the second page of the article.
   - (B) In the top right hand corner four lines from the top of the page, type the running head.
   - (C) Centered two lines below the running head is the page number. (Note that the page number and the running head will appear on each page of the paper in this location).
   - (D) Eight lines below the page number the word, ABSTRACT, is centered in capital letters.
   - (E) Four lines below the word ABSTRACT, type the abstract as a single paragraph in block format (without paragraph indentation).
   - (F) If your abstract is very long, it may be typed single-spaced.
   - (G) The abstract (and all other parts of the research paper) is typed in third person, past tense, passive voice.

RUNNING HEAD ———————————————→ Delinquency

PAGE NUMBER ———————————————→ 2.

HEADING ——————→ ABSTRACT

One hundred twenty subjects from a non-metropolitan South
Georgia area were studied to determine father-child relationship, and its subsequent influence on juvenile delinquency.
The sample consisted of sixty non-adjudicated and sixty
adjudicated juvenile delinquents. Their responses indicated
a strong relationship between the father role and juvenile
delinquency. The relationship found in the non-metropolitan
community was stronger and showed a higher level of significance than had been indicated in similar studies conducted
in major metropolitan areas. Differences in responses from
a contingency table analysis were established for the variables
paternal control, paternal affection, father absence, paternal
rejection, and the social model presented by the father. A
companion regression analysis established the variables
paternal affection, paternal rejection, social model presented
by the father, and father absence as significant indicators
of delinquent behavior in juveniles. It was concluded that
the role of the father in the non-metropolitan community is
a significant factor in the determination of delinquent
behavior in juveniles.

Introduction

1. The function of the introduction is to inform the
      reader of the specific problem or issue being
      studied.
2. The body of the introduction contains the following
      four subsections.
      A. Problem or issue being studied
            1. The problem might be presented in the
            form of a question (*i.e.,* What are the
            attitudes of South Georgians toward
            pornography?).
      B. Review of the literature
            1. Citations are used within the body of
                  the paper to make reference to
                  previous works. Indirect citations
                  are used when the researcher wishes
                  to place little emphasis on the
                  article cited. Direct citations are
                  used when the researcher wishes to
                  place greater emphasis on the
                  article cited.
            2. The researcher should cite only those
                  selected studies pertinent to the specific
                  issue or problem being studied.
            3. References with tangential or general
                  relevance should be avoided.
            4. Controversial issues should be treated
                  fairly. The researcher must be as
                  objective as possible and present both
                  (all) sides of an argument in the review
                  of the literature. To present only one
                  point of view is to propagandize.
            5. Do not cite a work older than ten years
                  unless it could be characterized as one of
                  the classics of that area.

Delinquency

3.

THE FATHER AND JUVENILE DELINQUENCY
IN A NON-METROPOLITAN COMMUNITY ←——— TITLE

All human groups, past and present, have apparently singled
out some of their members as "outsiders," "wicked," or flawed
in some way. No society has existed without deviants as well
as non-deviants. In modern American society negative social
responses are frequently directed at persons who are judged
by their peers to be alcoholics, criminals, mentally ill,
mentally subnormal, or given to bizarre sexual practices
(Liazos, 1972). ...cause of delinquent behavior.   ...In
regard to this, the problem was formulated as "What is the
influence of the father upon delinquent behavior in the non-
metropolitan community?" The responses of juveniles was
deemed worthy of research.

PROBLEM

Delinquency

4.

Under these circumstances juveniles indicated and over-
whelming tendency toward delinquent behavior (McCord, 1974).

The most comprehensive study concerning juvenile
delinquency was that of the Gluecks in Chicago. They
compared 500 offenders and 500 non-offenders, all under
the age of eighteen. They found...   In their study,
40% of the male offenders had affectionate father as
opposed to 81% of the male non-offenders (Glueck and
Glueck, 1950).

INDIRECT
CITATIONS

Delinquency

5.

A study by Rodman and Grams (1973) indicated that family background plays a major role in influencing juvenile delinquency. Sutherland and Cressy (1948) in their theory of differential association found that the social setting plays a major role as an indicator of deviant behavior.

DIRECT
CITATIONS

C. Operational definitions and the hypotheses
    1. Operational definitions are used to
        assign measurable meaning to an
        abstract concept or variable by
        specifying the activities or
        operations necessary to empirically
        measure the variable. All
        operational definitions should
        follow the review of the literature.
    2. The hypotheses state the expectations
        of the researcher concerning the
        problem being studied. In the
        hypotheses the researcher identifies
        the variables which he or she
        predicts will account for the
        results.
        a. Hypotheses should result from the
        review of the literature.
        b. Never introduce an hypothesis
        that has not been suggested by the
        review of the literature.
    3. Two types of hypotheses are:
        a. The null hypothesis (Ho) - this
        is a statistical statement of no
        relationship or no difference. It is
        an arbitrary convention
        hypothesizing that any relationship
        or difference in the findings is due
        to chance or sampling error and puts
        this supposition to a probability
        test. In theory, the null hypothesis
        is established for possible
        rejection. When rejected, the
        researcher can assume that
        differences do exist. He or she then
        proceeds to test the alternative
        hypotheses.
        b. The alternative (research)
        hypothesis (Ha) - this is the
        researcher's prediction of the
        outcome of the research study.

4. Testing the null hypothesis will result
in one of two outcomes:
a. The null hypothesis will be
accepted as true and the alternative
rejected.
b. The null will be rejected and the
alternative accepted as true.

Delinquency

6.

Operational Definitions:

   Adjudicated delinquent - a youth under the age of

      18 years who has been formally processed through

      the youth court system.

   Non-adjudicated juveniles - a youth under the age of

      18 years who has not been processed by the youth

      court system (even though hidden delinquency may

      exist).

   The review of the literature suggested the following

hypotheses:

   H_0: The role of the father has no influence upon

      delinquent behavior in juveniles.

   H_1: Paternal affection will influence delinquent

      behavior in juveniles.

   H_2: Father absence has an influence on juvenile

      delinquency.

NONDIRECTIONAL   NULL
ALTERNATIVE HYPOTHESES   HYPOTHESIS

D. Theoretical frame of reference (TFR)

    1.Every research project in the criminal justice domain must be grounded in a theoretical frame of reference. This can be a published model or a model created especially for the research project.

    2. The purpose of the TFR is to explain the predictive relationship between the variables from previous theoretical models. Consequently, the TFR is closely related to the hypotheses. Variables included in the hypotheses should be included in the TFR. It is possible for the TFR to apply established paradigms and suggest additional variables to be examined.

    3. When no established theoretical model can be used, the researcher may wish to construct one of his or her own. In its simplest form a predictive 2 x 2 model can serve as a TFR. Many will find this too limiting and experiment with a 2 x 2 x 3 (or larger) predictive model. This format is useful when typologies are suggested that organize and explain the research variables.

    4. The TFR should be exhaustive of all theoretical possibilities.

Delinquency

7.

Hirschi's (1969) theory of social control provided the theoretical framework for this study. The central thesis of this social control theory is that juveniles are free to commit delinquent acts when their ties to the conventional social order are broken. Hirschi's formulation of social control theory centered on the concept of bond, which referred to an individual's ties to behavioral standards that identify proper conduct. Hirschi identified several dimensions along which bond, or social control, varies. Attachment describes the strength of ties to others, such as family or peers. If the family fails to establish strong positive bonds with the child, the child will feel less attachment and seek behavioral models elsewhere.

THEORETICAL FRAME OF REFERENCE (T.F.R.)

3. Typing Instructions
    A. The introduction begins on a separate page
        from the abstract.
    B. The running head (as on every page) and the
        page number will be typed in the upper
        right hand corner in the same position as
        on the abstract page.
    C. The title of the paper is centered and typed
        in capital letters approximately eight
        lines below the page number.
    D. Four lines below the title the introduction
        begins in paragraph form.
    E. The introduction includes four subsections
        that follow each other. The author will be
        careful to develop appropriate
        transitional statements so that each
        subsection flows smoothly to the next.
    F. When the TFR is not written in paragraph
        form, it is possible to use a paradigm or
        representational figure to illustrate the
        theory being suggested. When such a
        paradigm is used, it is appropriate to
        include an explanatory paragraph in the
        text.

Delinquency

8.

This discussion of Hirschi's theory can be illustrated with the following representational paradigm:

S O C I A L   C O N T R O L

		LOW	HIGH
T			
Y		CHRONIC DELINQUENT	SITUATIONAL DELINQUENT
P	ADJUDICATED	a) Little Paternal affection	a) Neutral parental affection
E	DELINQUENT	b) High Paternal absence	b) Irregular parental absence
O		c) Poor paternal role modeling	c) Neutral role modeling
F			
Y	NON-ADJUDI-CATED YOUTH	HIDDEN DELINQUENT	NON-DELINQUENT
O		a) Neutral paternal affection	a) Great parental affection
U		b) Neutral role modeling	b) Little father absence
T		c) Irregular parental absence	c) positive role modeling
H			

↑

PARADIGM

Methods

1. The purpose of the method section is to tell the reader how the study was conducted. The method section should be described in enough detail to permit the study to be replicated. This material should allow the reader to evaluate the appropriateness of the methods and the probable reliability of the results.

2. The method section is divided into labeled subsections for the convenience of the reader. These subsections usually include, but are not limited to, the following: the subjects, the materials or apparatus, and the procedure.

   A. The Unit of Analysis

      1. Include a description of who or what was studied.

      2. Answer the following questions:

         a. How many cases were there?

         b. Who or what were the cases?

         c. What were the major characteristics of the cases? For example, describe people in terms of age, sex, race. Describe police departments in terms of size, organizational structure.

   B. The Materials and/or Apparatus

      1. Include a brief description of the materials used or the apparatus employed and their function in the project.

      2. Standardized materials or apparatus can usually be mentioned without great detail. However, specialized materials or equipment should be carefully identified.

      3. If an instrument was used, indicate where a copy can be found. If original, include in an Appendix. If published, simply indicate name, address, and catalog number of the item. If apparatus are used, include a photograph or a drawing of the apparatus.

   C. Procedures

      1. Discuss the method by which the instrument (if used) was validated. Indicate the results of any pretest.

2. Summarize each step of the research including the following:
   a. How were cases selected?
   b. How were data collected?
   c. How were data analyzed?
   d. What is the established level of statistical significance.
3. Typing Instructions
   a. The word METHODS is typed in capital letters, centered on the page four lines below the last sentence of the introduction.
   b. Two lines below the heading (METHOD), enter the subheading "Subjects" (if people served as the unit of analysis) at the left hand margin. Complete the information in paragraph form. Then enter the subheading, Materials, or Apparatus and complete that information in paragraph form. Finally, enter the subheading, Procedure, and enter the information that will allow the reader to replicate this study in paragraph form.

Delinquency

9.

If the family fails to establish strong positive bonds
with the children, the child may feel less attachment
and seek behavioral models elsewhere.

METHODS

Subjects: One hudnred twenty youth from non-metropolitan
South Georgia were studied. Sixty non-adjudicated youth
from area high schools comprised the control group. The
experimental group consisted of sixty adjudicated
delinquents from South Georgia Youth Community Treatment
Centers in Brunswick, Thomasville, Albany, and Savannah.
The subject's ages ranged from 13 to 18 years with an
average age of 16 years. In the control group there
were 39 males and 21 females. Of these, 63% were white
and 36% were black. The experimental group consisted
of 50 males and 10 females. Of these, 16% were white
and 83% were black.

Materials: A questionnaire consisting of 24 structured
questions was developed and administered to the two
groups. A copy will be found in the Appendix.

Delinquency

10.

<u>Procedure:</u> The independent variables were identified as
age, sex, race, family income, paternal control, paternal
affection, father absence, paternal rejection, and the
father's social role model. The dependent variable was
identified as juvenile delinquency. A preliminary form
of the instrument was pretested. As a result of the
pretest findings some questions were reworded to insure
validity. Subjects for the control group were randomly
selected and the instrument administered to them in their
high school classrooms. Subjects for the experimental
group were selected by directors of the area community
treatment centers to volunteer participants from non-
metropolitan Georgia. As a condition of the permission
to study adjudicated delinquents in the youth correction
system as set forth by a representative of the Gerogia
Department of Human Resources, Division of Information
Management, instruments were administered by the staff
members of the various centers. The data analysis
examined frequencies, a contingency table analysis, and
a regression analysis. The level of statistical
significance was established at .05.

Results

1. The Results is a summary of the collected data and
   a discussion of the statistical analysis.
   - A. Present a brief summary of the grouped data
     in paragraph form. This discussion
     typically will explain the tables of data
     found in the Appendix. However, the
     paragraph explanation of the tables must
     each stand alone.
   - B. The construction of tables that are clean,
     clearly labeled, and concise is important.
     The tables most often included include a
     frequency table, summary significance
     tables, a correlation table, and other
     tables as needed. Three to five tables are
     typically needed to summarize the col-
     lected data and the statistical analysis.
   - C. For each table in the Appendix, there should
     be a paragraph in the results section.
2. Typing Instructions
   - A. The word RESULTS is typed in capital
     letters and centered on the page four
     lines below the last line of the previous
     method section.
   - B. Two lines below the heading (RESULTS) type
     the text of this section in paragraph
     form.

Delinquency

·11.

RESULTS

Table 1 summarized the descriptive statistics for
the background variables. A typical member of the sample
was found to be between sixteen and eighteen years of
age, from a family whose income ranged from $6,000.00 to
$25,000.00 per year. ...While the control group
reflected the general demographic statistics for the
area, the experimental group averaged significantly more
males and blacks, lower educational levels, and larger
family sizes.

Table II summarized the findings of the contingency
table analysis and ordered the significant variables as:
paternal affection, paternal rejection, father's role
model, paternal control, and father absence.

Discussion

1. The discussion section of an article is the portion
   in which the author is free to examine,
   interpret, draw inferences, and qualify the
   findings. This should be done in respect to the
   hypotheses.
2. Steps in writing a discussion section are:
   A. Begin with a clear statement of the support
      or non-support of each null hypothesis. If
      the null hypothesis is not accepted, then
      summarize the support for each alternative
      (research) hypothesis.
   B. Identify each significant indicator and
      discuss in terms of the findings. Be sure
      to suggest what each means and how each is
      related to the other significant findings.
   C. Show how the findings relate to the work of
      other authors who have studied a similar
      problem. Discuss why there is agreement or
      disagreement with these cited studies.
   D. Discuss how these findings relate to the
      Theoretical Frame of Reference. Show how
      the findings amplify the theory.
   E. Demonstrate the relevance and possible policy
      implications of the results to the sample
      studied and for the general population.
   F. Explore the implications of any serendipitous
      findings and their implications to the
      problem being studied.
   G. Suggest improvements to the research design
      for future research in this problem area.
   H. While it is optional, a short paragraph of
      conclusions will often help the reader
      draw together the summary of your project.
3. Typing Instructions
   A. The word DISCUSSION is typed in capital
      letters and centered on the page four
      lines below the last sentence of the
      results section.
   B. Two lines below the heading (DISCUSSION)
      begin the text in paragraph form.

Delinquency

12.

Paternal affection, paternal rejection, father absence,
and to a lesser extent paternal control indicated delinquent
behavior in juveniles.

DISCUSSION

The null hypothesis was not accepted. Numerous
significant findings from the contingency table analysis
lead the researcher to accept the alternative hypotheses
(H_1-H_5) which stated that paternal affection, father
absence, paternal control, paternal rejection, and father's
role model would influence juvenile delinquency. A
detailed examination of each suggested the following
effects:

Paternal Affection:

The degree of paternal affection overwhelmingly
indicated that juvenile delinquency is directly re-

Reference Section

1. This is a list of books and articles which
     documents the statements made in the article.
     Any work cited in the article must appear in the
     reference section of the paper. Each entry in
     the reference list must appear in the text of
     the research paper.

2. Typing Instructions

     A. The references begin on a separate page
          following the discussion section.

     B. The word REFERENCES is typed in all capital
          letters, centered twelve lines down from
          the top of the page.

     C. Entries are arranged in alphabetical order by
          the surname of the author.

     D. Arrange the elements in a reference entry in
          the following order:

          1. Author: enter all authors of the work,
               with surname(s) and initials (not
               full names) in inverted order.

          2. Title: type the title exactly as it
               appears in the work cited.

          3. Facts of publication:

               a. journals - complete name of the
                    journal, date of publication, volume
                    number, inclusive pages.

               b. books - place of publication (followed by a
                    colon), publisher's name, and date
                    of publication.

     E. Punctuation

          1. Periods follow the author, title, and
               publication date.

          2. Commas follow the author's surname(s),
               and all other entries. If the list
               of authors is long, semi-colons may
               be substituted for commas for
               clarity.

     F. Capitalization

          1. Capitalize the first word in a title,
               and the first word after a colon in
               a title.

          2. Capitalize the first letter of each
               word in a journal title, the

publisher's name, and all proper
nouns.

Delinquency

21.

REFERENCES

Becker, H.S. <u>Outsiders</u>. New York: The Free Press,
    1963.

Boone, S.L. Effects of father absence and birth order
    on aggressive behavior in young male children.
    <u>Psychological Reports</u>, 1979, 44, 1223-1229.

Cavenar, J.O. and Butts, N.T. Unconscious communication
    between father and son. <u>American Journal of</u>
    <u>Psychiatry</u>, 1979, 136, 344-345.

Gibbons, D.C. <u>Delinquent behavior</u>. Englewood Cliffs:
    Prentice-Hall, Inc., 1970.

Grinnell, R. and Chambers, C. Broken homes and middle-
    class delinquency: A comparison. <u>Criminology</u>,
    1979, 17, 395-400.

Appendices
1. Use a separate title page for each Appendix and
    label each either A, B, C, D. etc.
2. Use only appendices as required by the
    documentation of the text.
3. Appendices should include:
    A. The Tables
    B. Supporting evidence not published elsewhere
    C. The Instrument

This is the last section in the paper. Students are reminded that the examples given are incomplete. They are just to suggest the proper form and were taken from an undergraduate student paper. For best results in writing, the student is urged to read journal articles regularly and to consult the *Style Manual of the American Psychological Association* or other appropriate style guide whenever questions arise.

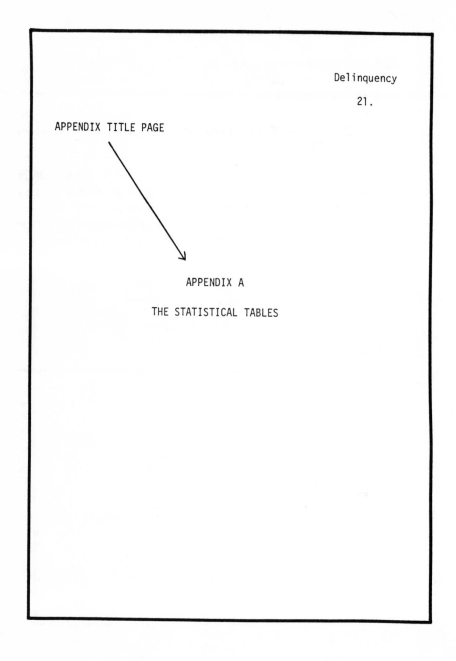

Delinquency

21.

APPENDIX TITLE PAGE

APPENDIX A

THE STATISTICAL TABLES

Delinquency

22.

TABLE 1

FREQUENCY ANALYSIS

		N	Percent
Age:	13-15 years	30	25%
	16-17	79	66
	18 and over	11	9
		120	100%
Sex:	Male	89	75%
	Female	31	25
		120	100%
Race:	Black	52	44%
	White	61	50
	Oriental	3	3
	Hispanic	4	3
		120	100%
Educ. Level:	6th Grade	7	5%
	7th	11	9
	8th	29	25
	9th	38	32
	10th	22	18
	11th	12	10
	high school graduate	2	1
		120	100%

The Oral Presentation

Prior to publication and often before a research manuscript is submitted to a journal for consideration, the research is often presented at a professional meeting. This provides an opportunity for the researcher's colleagues to raise questions so that the product can be refined. The major professional societies at which research in the field of ciminal justice is presented are the Academy of Criminal Justice Sciences and the American Society of Criminology. Presentations at these meetings can be unnerving to the student the first few times that he or she participates. The typical format for presentation of a paper at these meetings consists of a panel of three to five presenters with papers on related topics. The panel chair will allot a block of time to each presenter (usually 15 or 20 minutes) and a discussant will often be assigned to critique the papers after all have been presented. Finally, the audience will be provided with the opportunity to ask questions and offer commentary. The following ideas are offered to aid in the preparation of an oral presentation of research:

1. The presentation must be kept brief. It is important not to exceed the allotted time because doing so will infringe on the time of other presenters, the discussant and/or audience participation.
2. Prepare handouts of the tables or disseminate copies of the paper. The audience will have difficulty following statistical analyses without these aids.
3. Suggest the problem, method, and main findings. Usually there is a question and answer period in which members of the audience will ask about specifics.
4. Try to be enthusiastic. Remember that you probably know more about this research than anyone else. This is your opportunity to share your special knowledge.
5. Be prepared. Never "wing" a project report or speak "off the cuff." This is no time for unending monologue or reading a paper verbatim. The presentation should be practiced several times prior to delivery.
6. The following brief outline can serve as a general guide to a presentation.

I. The Problem
    a. Why is this important?
    b. Why did you choose to study it?
    c. What meaning does it have for the field?
II. The Background Research
    a. Who has studied this problem in the past?
    b. What have they found?
III. The Method
    a. How were the data gathered?
    b. Was the data collection technique valid,
        reliable, and representative?
    c. Describe the unit of analysis and the cases.
    d. What procedures did you follow?
    e. How were the data analyzed?
IV. What were the main findings?
V. Has theory been amplified?
VI. What were problems and limitations? What direction
    can be suggested for future research?

References

American Psychological Association *Publication Manual of The American Psychological Association*, Third Edition (Washington, D.C.: American Psychological Association, 1983).

Index